ITALY
SEA
TO SKY

URSULA FERRIGNO

ITALY
SEA
TO SKY

FOOD OF THE ISLANDS, COASTS,
RIVERS, MOUNTAINS, FORESTS
AND PLAINS

PHOTOGRAPHS BY JASON LOWE

MITCHELL BEAZLEY

Italy: Sea to Sky

by Ursula Ferrigno

First published in Great Britain in 2003 by Mitchell Beazley, an imprint of
Octopus Publishing Group Limited,
2–4 Heron Quays, London E14 4JP

ISBN 1 84000 600 5

A CIP catalogue record for this book is available from the British Library. The
author and publisher will be grateful for any information that will assist them
in keeping future editions up to date. While all reasonable care has been taken
during the preparation of this book, neither the publisher, editors, nor the
author can accept liability for any consequences arising from the use thereof or
from the information contained therein.

Commissioning Editor: Rebecca Spry
Executive Art Editor: Yasia Williams
Design: Miranda Harvey
Editor: Susan Fleming
Photographer: Jason Lowe
Production: Alex McCulloch and Sheila Smith
Proofreader: Annie Lee
Index: John Noble

Typeset in Perpetua and TradeGothic

Printed and bound by Toppan Printing Company in China

NOTE
All eggs are organic, free-range and the largest you can find. Organic
vegetables are best too.

Dedication
For the honourable, flavoursome Richard

Acknowledgements

Rebecca Spry For pursuing this project and shaping
it into a fantastically different book. I'm thrilled
with the result. You have great talent and are a
huge source of fun. Thank you.

Susan Fleming The only editor for me. Your
knowledge, integrity, intelligence and dedication
make you a one-off. You are a generous soul, with
a great sense of fun and energy. I couldn't have
managed this book without you. Thank you for
working with me again.

Jason Lowe Yet again sensational photography.
Thank you for exploring such interesting angles to
make this book stand out from the crowd.

Miranda Harvey So good to work with you in Italy.
Thank you for your design; your excellence and
talent have contributed an exciting and thought-
provoking aspect to my book.

Rosie and Eric of Books for Cooks Thank you for
your continual support – you are a remarkable
inspiration to us all.

contents

I AM PASSIONATE ABOUT ITALY – ABOUT HER VARIED LANDSCAPES AND CLIMATES, HER RICH CULTURE, THE WARMTH OF HER PEOPLE AND, INEVITABLY, HER FOOD. EVERY TYPE OF ITALIAN FOOD FILLS MY SENSES, FROM THE OLIVE OILS AND CHEESES TO THE PASTAS AND RISOTTOS. I'M CAPTIVATED BY THE COUNTRY'S LIVELY FLAVOURS. I LOVE MANY TYPES OF FOOD, BUT FOR ME THE ITALIAN KITCHEN IS STILL THE MOST EXCITING PLACE TO BE.

THE COOKING STYLE THROUGHOUT ITALY IS SIMPLE AND BASIC, AND THE INGREDIENTS USED ARE LOCAL, SEASONAL AND DELICIOUSLY FRESH. AS A TEACHER, I'M ALWAYS DELIGHTED TO DEMONSTRATE HOW TO MAKE OUR SIMPLE DISHES, AND MY STUDENTS ARE OFTEN SURPRISED BY HOW STRAIGHTFORWARD THE COOKING IS. BUT BOTH INGREDIENTS AND THE RECIPES FOR INDIVIDUAL DISHES CAN DIFFER FROM ONE PART OF THE COUNTRY TO ANOTHER. THIS IS PARTLY BECAUSE OF THE ASTOUNDING FACT THAT IT IS LESS THAN 150 YEARS SINCE ITALY CONSISTED OF A SERIES OF INDIVIDUAL CITY STATES OR REGIONS, EACH OF WHICH HAD DEVELOPED A LOCAL STYLE OF COOKING THAT WAS SOMETIMES MARGINALLY, SOMETIMES RADICALLY DIFFERENT FROM THAT OF ITS NEIGHBOURS. ANOTHER REASON FOR THIS REGIONAL DIVERSITY IS THAT

VARIOUS PARTS OF ITALY HAVE BEEN INFLUENCED BY OTHER NATIONS – BY PEACEFUL OR AGGRESSIVE INVADERS WHO BROUGHT WITH THEM THEIR OWN INGREDIENTS, CULINARY IDEAS AND STYLES. THE ORIGINAL TEMPLATE OF ITALY'S COOKING HAS BEEN EMBELLISHED AND OVERLAID OVER THE CENTURIES BY IDEAS FROM THE GREEKS, ROMANS, ARABS, FRENCH AND SPANISH.

BUT, OF COURSE – AND THIS IS THE *RAISON D'ÊTRE* OF THIS BOOK – GEOGRAPHY HAS PLAYED THE MOST IMPORTANT ROLE IN THE DEVELOPMENT OF LOCAL STYLES OF COOKING. FOR THOSE LIVING ON THE LONG COASTLINES OF ITALY, SEAFOOD IS A MAJOR INGREDIENT; FOR THOSE WITH NO ACCESS TO THE SEA, THE EQUIVALENT SOURCE OF PROTEIN WOULD BE IMPORTED PRESERVED FISH. FOR ITALIANS LIVING IN THE HEAT OF THE SOUTH, SUN-LOVING VEGETABLES WOULD BE EVERYDAY FOODS; FOR THEIR NORTHERN COMPATRIOTS, CARBOHYDRATE-RICH PASTA, BEANS AND POLENTA WOULD KEEP THE MOUNTAIN CHILLS AT BAY DURING WINTER. ITALY'S COASTLINES, HER WOODS AND FORESTS, PLAINS, MOUNTAINS, LAKES, RIVERS AND ISLANDS, ALL CONTRIBUTE TO THE RICHNESS AND DIVERSITY OF THE COUNTRY'S LOCALLY-BASED CUISINE. THIS HAS BEEN PART OF MY CONSCIOUSNESS SINCE MY CHILDHOOD, AND I CELEBRATE IT HERE WITH ALL MY HEART.

introduction

monthene
mountains

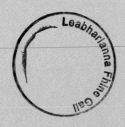

ITALY IS ALMOST ENTIRELY COMPOSED OF MOUNTAINS. THE APENNINES FORM THE COUNTRY'S SPINE, RUNNING FROM PIEDMONT IN THE NORTH RIGHT DOWN TO CALABRIA, THE TOE OF THE ITALIAN 'BOOT', IN THE SOUTH. AT ITALY'S NORTHERN BORDERS, THE DOLOMITES RISE BETWEEN THE COUNTRY AND ITS NEIGHBOURS AUSTRIA AND SWITZERLAND, AND THE AOSTA VALLEY (THE SMALLEST REGION) LIES IN THE ALPS.

ITALY'S MOUNTAINS ARE BREATHTAKINGLY BEAUTIFUL, AND WHEREVER YOU ARE THEY FORM A BACKDROP TO VIRTUALLY EVERYTHING. THE MEDIEVAL TUSCAN TOWN OF LUCCA, FOR INSTANCE, OUTLINED AGAINST THE DRAMATICALLY SERRATED SKYLINE FORMED BY THE APENNINES, EMPHASISES THE SMALLNESS OF MAN'S ACHIEVEMENT WHEN COMPARED TO THE GRANDEUR OF NATURE. BUT THAT GRANDEUR CAN BE BLEAK AND VIOLENT TOO, PARTICULARLY IN THE SOUTH. THE APENNINES WERE FORMED BY VOLCANIC ACTION AND THE FAULT LINE IS STILL ACTIVE – THINK OF VESUVIUS AND MOUNT ETNA IN SICILY, RIGHT AT THE END OF THE RANGE. WHEN I WAS IN PERUGIA ONCE THERE WAS A MINOR EARTHQUAKE THAT CAUSED MUCH DAMAGE.

IN OTHER COUNTRIES MOUNTAINOUS AREAS MIGHT BE LEFT TO NATURE, BUT IN ITALY NO TRACT OF LAND, HOWEVER DUBIOUS ITS POTENTIAL AT FIRST GLANCE, IS WASTED, AND THE MOUNTAINSIDES HAVE BEEN PRESSED INTO SERVICE FOR CENTURIES, ALTHOUGH NEVER ENTIRELY TAMED. OLIVE GROVES RISE IN TERRACES, OFTEN AT DIZZYING HEIGHTS (PARTICULARLY IN LIGURIA), AND THE OLIVE FRUITS – LARGE AND SMALL; GREEN, PURPLE AND BLACK – ARE USED IN THE DISHES OF THE MOUNTAINS, ALONG WITH THEIR LUSCIOUS OIL. IN MANY REGIONS, VEGETABLES ARE GROWN BETWEEN THE BEAUTIFUL, GNARLED TREES, WASTING EVEN LESS SPACE. FRUIT ORCHARDS CLOTHE HIGH SLOPES WITH COLOUR AND FRAGRANCE AT BLOSSOM TIME, WHILE REGIMENTED LINES OF GRAPE VINES COVER THE FOOTHILLS BELOW.

IN THE HIGH VALLEYS, THE SCRUB AND PASTURES ARE MADE UP OF GRASSES AND WILD HERBS, THE

LATTER WITH AN AROMA SO INTENSE THAT YOU CAN SMELL IT AS YOU WALK. IN THE WILD HERB FIELDS THE GREATEST MOUNTAIN ACTIVITY TAKES PLACE: THE WORK OF THE HERDSMEN. AS SOON AS THE LAST SNOWS HAVE MELTED, HERDS OF COWS ARE TAKEN INTO THE ALPINE VALLEYS OF THE NORTH WHERE, ALL SPRING AND SUMMER, THEY CROP THE LUSH PASTURES. FONTINA FROM THE AOSTA VALLEY, GORGONZOLA FROM LOMBARDY, ASIAGO FROM THE VENETO, AND TALEGGIO AND TOMA ARE AMONG THE MANY CHEESES MADE. FURTHER SOUTH, WHERE THERE IS LESS GOOD PASTURE FOR COWS (ALTHOUGH COWS' MILK CHEESES ARE STILL MADE), SHEEP AND GOATS (AND BUFFALO, SEE PAGE 122) ARE MILKED IN THE MOUNTAINS TO PRODUCE SOME OF ITALY'S BEST CHEESES, AMONG THEM PECORINO AND ITS BY-PRODUCT, RICOTTA.

FOODS EATEN IN THE MOUNTAINS TEND TO BE RICHER IN CARBOHYDRATES THAN THOSE FOUND ELSEWHERE IN ITALY. THESE ARE SUSTAINING INGREDIENTS TO HELP THE BODY SURVIVE THE WINTER COLD. A LOT OF DRIED PASTA AND POLENTA IS EATEN, ALTHOUGH THEIR BASIC INGREDIENTS – WHEAT AND MAIZE – ARE GROWN IN THE PLAINS. IN FACT, MOUNTAIN RECIPES OFTEN DOUBLE UP ON CARBOHYDRATE, A CHARACTERISTIC OF THE COLDER NORTH. THE FOOD HERE IS SIMPLER THAN THAT PRODUCED ELSEWHERE IN ITALY – THINK OF PASTA WITH VEGETABLES OR CHEESE, VEGETABLES WITH CHEESE SAUCES OR POLENTA WITH CHEESE. THESE ARE COMBINATIONS OF FRUGAL INGREDIENTS TO MAKE A FLAVOURSOME WHOLE.

FOR ADDITIONAL FLAVOURINGS, PRESERVED FISH AND SALTED VEGETABLES ARE INCLUDED IN THE COOKING. ITALIANS FAR FROM THE SEA HAVE NO HISTORICAL CULTURE OF FRESH FISH EATING, SO THEY HAVE ALWAYS RELIED ON FOODS LIKE SALTED ANCHOVIES OR DRIED OR SALTED COD. HOWEVER, ABOVE ALL ELSE, EATING IN THE MOUNTAINS IS ASSOCIATED WITH HEALTH. IN FACT, THE AIR THERE IS SO PURE THAT ONE PASTA MANUFACTURER DRIED HIS PASTA THERE BECAUSE OF THE UNPOLLUTED ATMOSPHERE!

TO ME, THE MOST CHARACTERISTIC COLOUR OF ITALY IS THE SILVERY GREEN OF THE
OLIVE. THE TREES GROW IN MOST PARTS OF THE COUNTRY, USUALLY ON THE LOWER
SLOPES OF THE MOUNTAINS. IN LIGURIA THE TREES ARE GROWN IN TERRACES SO
STEEP THAT THEY CAN ONLY BE REACHED BY FOOT.

THE OLIVE FRUIT HAS BEEN VALUED IN ITALY FOR CENTURIES. THE QUALITY OF
THE OIL DEPENDS ON THE TYPE OF TREE, THE RIPENESS OF THE FRUIT, THE CLIMATE,
THE LOCATION AND THE SOIL. MOST OIL IS PRESSED FROM UNRIPE GREEN OLIVES
(THEY BECOME PURPLE AND BLACK AS THEY MATURE). TUSCAN OIL IS CONSIDERED
PRECIOUS BECAUSE THE OLIVES ARE PICKED EARLY, YIELDING AN OIL THAT IS HIGH ON
FLAVOUR BUT LOW ON VOLUME. CONVERSELY, THE LIGURIAN TAGGIASCA OLIVES ARE
PICKED AND PRESSED WHEN ALMOST RIPE.

OLIVES TO BE EATEN ARE GENERALLY DIFFERENT VARIETIES FROM THOSE PRESSED
FOR OIL, WITH THE EXCEPTION OF TAGGIASCA. THEY ARE INEDIBLE STRAIGHT OFF THE
TREE, WHETHER GREEN OR BLACK, AND HAVE TO BE BRINED OR SALTED FIRST. THE
SMALL WRINKLED BLACK OLIVES FROM GAETA, NEAR NAPLES, ARE THE BEST.

olive e acciughe

OLIVES AND ANCHOVIES

I WAS FIRST INTRODUCED TO THIS DELICIOUS CONCOCTION IN UMBRIA. THE IDEA COMES FROM THE TOWN OF ASCOLI PICENO IN THE MARCHES, WHICH BORDERS ON UMBRIA. THE OLIVES THERE ARE HUGE. THE ONLY TIME-CONSUMING PART OF THIS RECIPE IS STONING THE OLIVES: SIT DOWN WITH A FRIEND AND A GLASS OF WINE AND GET ON WITH IT WHILE CHATTING.

olive ascolane

STUFFED OLIVES

SERVES 4 AS AN ANTIPASTO

85G (3OZ) SALTED CAPERS, RINSED AND
    FINELY CHOPPED
1 SMALL GARLIC CLOVE, PEELED AND CRUSHED
125G (4½OZ) FRESH BREADCRUMBS
A HANDFUL OF FRESH FLAT-LEAF PARSLEY,
    FINELY CHOPPED
SEA SALT AND FRESHLY GROUND BLACK PEPPER
OLIVE OIL
12 VERY LARGE GREEN OLIVES
    (QUEEN OLIVES), STONED
1 TBSP ITALIAN '00' PLAIN FLOUR
1 LARGE FREE-RANGE EGG, BEATEN

1 Put the capers, garlic, half the breadcrumbs, parsley, and some salt and pepper into a bowl and mix together. Add a little olive oil to bind.

2 Using a piping bag fitted with a small plain nozzle, stuff the olives with the mixture.

3 Put the flour, beaten egg and remaining breadcrumbs on separate small plates. Roll the olives in the flour first, then the egg, then the breadcrumbs.

4 Heat about 2 tbsp of olive oil in a frying pan and fry the olives until golden brown. Serve hot or cold.

pane di olive con cipolla farcita

OLIVE BREAD WITH ONION FILLING

SERVES 6-8 GENEROUSLY

DOUGH

15G (½OZ) FRESH YEAST

275ML (9½FL OZ) WARM WATER, AT BLOOD
    TEMPERATURE

500G (1LB 2OZ) STRONG FLOUR OR ITALIAN
    '00' FLOUR

5G (¼OZ) SALT

2 TBSP OLIVE OIL, PLUS EXTRA FOR OILING

70G (2½OZ) OLIVES, THE BEST YOU CAN GET,
    STONED, SLICED AND DRAINED

FILLING

2 TBSP OLIVE OIL

3 RED ONIONS, PEELED AND CHOPPED

2 BAY LEAVES

1 SPRIG FRESH ROSEMARY, LEAVES PICKED
    FROM THE STALKS

2 TBSP RED WINE VINEGAR

55G (2OZ) SOFT BROWN SUGAR

TO FINISH

A FEW FRESH ROSEMARY LEAVES

OLIVE OIL

ROCK SALT

1   To start the dough, dissolve the yeast in the warm water in a small bowl.

2   Sieve the flour on to a work surface and make a well in the centre. Add the salt and olive oil. Gradually add the yeast solution and incorporate the flour to form a dough. Knead the dough by hand for 10-15 minutes, until smooth and elastic.

3   Add the olives and continue kneading until they are evenly distributed. Lightly oil a bowl large enough to allow the dough to double in bulk. Put the dough in the bowl and cover with a cloth. Leave for 40 minutes.

4   Meanwhile, to make the onion filling, heat the olive oil and add the onions, bay leaves and rosemary. Brown the onions well over a low-to-medium heat, stirring regularly to prevent sticking. Add the vinegar and stir well to deglaze the pan. Finally add the sugar and cook over a low heat for 30 minutes. The mixture should be thick, shiny and rich red in colour. Cool completely. (This filling can be made in advance and kept in the fridge for a couple of days.)

5   Knock back the dough, divide in two and shape each piece of dough into a ball. Leave to relax for 10 minutes.

6   Using a rolling pin, roll each ball out into a long flat oval shape. Place half the onion mixture and a few extra rosemary leaves slightly off-centre in each half of the dough. Fold each

piece over and pinch the edges together. Lightly brush the tops with olive oil and sprinkle over some rock salt and rosemary leaves.

7   Place the two dough pieces on a lightly greased baking tray and prove for 40 minutes. Meanwhile, preheat the oven to 200°C (400°F) gas mark 6.

8   Bake the breads for 25 minutes, until golden brown. Remove from the oven, brush with olive oil and cool on a wire rack.

ROASTED AND STUFFED PEPPERS ARE ASSOCIATED WITH PIEDMONT, BUT THIS VERSION IS MUCH MORE SOUTHERN, WITH ITS USE OF ANCHOVIES, CAPERS, OLIVES AND ARTICHOKES. I INVENTED THIS RECIPE WHEN COOKING LUNCH FOR FRIENDS ONE LAZY SUNDAY MORNING.

peperoni arrosto con carciofi, pecorino e noci

ROAST PEPPERS WITH ARTICHOKES, PECORINO AND NUTS

SERVES 6

6 ARTICHOKES

1 LEMON, HALVED

A FEW FRESH THYME SPRIGS

4 GARLIC CLOVES, PEELED AND CRUSHED

3 TBSP OLIVE OIL

400ML (14FL OZ) WATER

2 RED PEPPERS

1 YELLOW PEPPER

55G (2OZ) SHELLED WALNUTS

250G (9OZ) PECORINO SARDO CHEESE, CUT INTO
   1CM (½IN) DICE, PLUS EXTRA FOR SHAVINGS

4 ANCHOVIES, DRAINED

1 TBSP SALTED CAPERS, RINSED

2 TBSP STONED BLACK OLIVES (OPTIONAL)

A HANDFUL OF FRESH FLAT-LEAF PARSLEY,
   CHOPPED

2 TBSP EXTRA VIRGIN OLIVE OIL

SEA SALT AND FRESHLY GROUND BLACK PEPPER

1 Preheat the oven to 200°C (400°F) gas mark 6. Trim the artichokes down to the heart, keeping a portion of the tender stem, and quarter them. Rub the cut artichokes with half of the lemon to keep them from darkening.

2 Place the artichokes in a deep-sided sauté pan. Add the thyme sprigs, garlic and the other lemon half. Cover the artichokes with the olive oil and water, bring them to a simmer and cook for about 15 minutes, until tender. Strain the artichokes.

3 Roast the peppers in the preheated oven for 20 minutes, until they are blistered all over, then leave to cool. Halve the peppers lengthways, then peel and remove the stems and seeds. Arrange the pepper halves, peeled side down, on a serving platter.

4 Place the artichokes, walnuts, cheese dice, anchovies, capers, olives and parsley in a bowl. Add the extra virgin olive oil and some salt and pepper. Spoon the mixture over the peppers and garnish with pecorino shavings.

ANCHOVIES, GARLIC AND OLIVE OIL – INGREDIENTS USED IN THE TRADITIONAL WARM
DIPPING SAUCE, *BAGNA CAUDA* – WERE ORIGINALLY BROUGHT TO PIEDMONT FROM
THE COASTAL REGION OF LIGURIA. *BAGNA CAUDA*, WHICH MEANS 'HOT BATH' IN THE
PIEDMONTESE DIALECT, IS USUALLY SERVED AS A DIP WITH CRISP RAW VEGETABLES.

peperoni con bagna cauda

PEPPERS IN A HOT BATH

SERVES 4

4 SWEET AND TENDER YELLOW PEPPERS

6 LARGE GARLIC CLOVES, UNPEELED

10-12 SALTED ANCHOVIES, RINSED, FILLETED
    AND FINELY CHOPPED

85ML (3FL OZ) OLIVE OIL (EXTRA VIRGIN IS TOO
    STRONG)

FRESHLY GROUND BLACK PEPPER TO TASTE

1   Preheat the oven to 150°C (300°F) gas mark 2.

2   Place the whole peppers on a baking sheet and roast for
    1 hour; rotate them after the first 30 minutes and then again
    after 15 minutes. The peppers should remain firm and hold
    their shape. If they begin to soften remove them from the
    oven immediately. Let the peppers cool slightly.

3   Cook the garlic cloves in a small pot of boiling water for
    20-30 minutes, or until they are very soft. Let the garlic cool,
    then peel and mash the pulp with a fork. Mash the anchovies
    into the garlic to make a smooth purée.

4   When the peppers are cool enough to handle, skin them. Cut
    the peppers in half lengthwise, core and seed them, then drain
    them, hollow-side-down, on kitchen paper.

5   Combine the garlic and anchovy purée with the olive oil and
    some black pepper in the top of a double boiler (or in a bowl
    over a pan). Cook the mixture over simmering water, stirring
    often, for 30 minutes.

6   Arrange the pepper halves, hollow-side-up, on a serving
    platter, spoon the warm sauce into the hollows, and serve
    immediately. The pepper halves can be reheated before filling
    with sauce if you prefer to serve them warm.

THESE BEAUTIFUL LITTLE PEPPER ROLLS MAY SEEM FIDDLY, BUT THEY'RE WELL
WORTH THE EFFORT. THE STRONG, TYPICALLY SOUTHERN FLAVOURS OF THE
OLIVES AND ANCHOVIES, COMBINED WITH THE JUICINESS OF THE PEPPERS,
MAKE THEM A REAL FAMILY FAVOURITE. THEY ARE WONDERFUL FOR LUNCH
SERVED SIMPLY WITH SOME FRESH BREAD WITH A CRISP GREEN SALAD AND
ARE EQUALLY GOOD FOR SHARING WITH FRIENDS AT A PARTY. WE EAT THEM AT
LEAST ONCE A WEEK AT HOME IN ITALY.

involtini di peperoni

SWEET PEPPER ROLLS WITH OLIVES, PINE NUTS AND ANCHOVIES

SERVES 4 AS AN ANTIPASTO

4 LARGE RED PEPPERS

4 TBSP FRESH BREADCRUMBS

55G (2OZ) GREEN OLIVES, STONED AND
    CHOPPED

2 TBSP PINE NUTS, TOASTED

55G (2OZ) ANCHOVIES, DRAINED AND CHOPPED

1 GARLIC CLOVE, PEELED AND CHOPPED

1 SPRIG FRESH FLAT-LEAF PARSLEY, FINELY
    CHOPPED

EXTRA VIRGIN OLIVE OIL

SEA SALT AND FRESHLY GROUND BLACK PEPPER

1 Under a very hot grill, blacken the peppers on all sides. Leave
   to cool, then peel. Cut in half lengthways and remove stems
   and seeds, trying to preserve the juice.

2 Mix together the breadcrumbs, olives, pine nuts, anchovies,
   garlic and parsley, and add enough olive oil and pepper juice
   to bind. Season to taste.

3 Put a tablespoon of filling in each half pepper and roll up.
   Cut each roll in small pieces and arrange on a serving dish.
   Serve hot or cold.

FENNEL HAS ESTABLISHED ITSELF AS A DELICIOUSLY VERSATILE VEGETABLE WELL BEYOND THE BOUNDARIES OF ITS NATIVE ITALY, WHERE IT IS EATEN RAW AS A *DIGESTIVO*. THIS IS THE IDEAL RECIPE FOR CONVERTING ANYONE WHO REMAINS UNCONVINCED BY FENNEL'S CHARMS.

bruschetta di finocchio, cipolla e olive

CARAMELISED FENNEL, ONION AND OLIVE BRUSCHETTA

SERVES 4

15G (½OZ) BUTTER

1 TBSP OLIVE OIL

2 ONIONS, PEELED AND FINELY SLICED

2 FENNEL BULBS, TRIMMED, QUARTERED AND
   FINELY SLICED

50ML (2FL OZ) WHITE WINE

8 BLACK OLIVES, STONED AND SLICED

SEA SALT AND FRESHLY GROUND BLACK PEPPER

4 LARGE SLICES OPEN-TEXTURED BREAD,
   CUT 1CM (½IN) THICK

1　Melt the butter and olive oil in a non-stick heavy-bottomed pan. Stir in the sliced onions and fennel, and stew slowly for about three-quarters of an hour, until the vegetables are golden brown and tender, stirring from time to time.

2　Add the wine and olives and continue cooking until the wine has bubbled away completely. Adjust the seasoning and keep the mixture warm.

3　Grill the bread until it is golden brown. Spoon over the warm fennel mixture and serve at once.

THIS RECIPE COMES FROM TUSCANY, HOME TO SOME WONDERFUL OLIVE OIL, AND IT IS FABULOUSLY EASY TO PREPARE. THE OLIVES USED ARE TOO RIPE TO BE PRESSED FOR OIL. I GIVE SMALL JARS OF THESE OLIVES TO FRIENDS AS GIFTS.

olive di montefiascone

MARINATED OLIVES

MAKES ABOUT 500G (1LB 2OZ)
500G (1LB 2OZ) BLACK OLIVES WITH STONES IN
PEEL OF 1 ORANGE AND 1 LEMON, CUT INTO
   MEDIUM PIECES
3 GARLIC CLOVES, PEELED AND CRUSHED
A HANDFUL OF FENNEL SEEDS, CRUSHED
COARSELY GROUND BLACK PEPPER TO TASTE
EXTRA VIRGIN OLIVE OIL

1 Place the olives in a bowl, and add the orange and lemon peel, garlic, fennel seeds and black pepper.

2 Mix well and place in a clean jar with a generous covering of olive oil. The olives will be deliciously infused after about 10 days.

ITALY HAS A WONDERFULLY DIVERSE RANGE OF CHEESES, AND MOST ARE EITHER MADE
IN THE MOUNTAINS BY INDIVIDUAL FAMILIES OR AT CHEESE PLANTS TO WHICH THE
MOUNTAIN MILK IS SENT. IN GENERAL, COWS' MILK CHEESES (GORGONZOLA,
PARMESAN, FONTINA AND MASCARPONE) ARE PRODUCED IN THE NORTH, AND EWES'
AND GOATS' MILK CHEESES (PECORINO, CAPRINO AND RICOTTA) FURTHER SOUTH,
ALONG WITH THE FAMOUS BUFFALO MILK CHEESE (MOZZARELLA, SEE PAGE 122).

ITALY'S SOFT CHEESES, PARTICULARLY MASCARPONE AND RICOTTA, ARE USED IN
DESSERTS (THINK OF TIRAMISU) AND IN RAVIOLI FILLINGS. GORGONZOLA, A BLUE
CHEESE, IS NOW PRODUCED IN FACTORIES, BUT IT IS STILL MATURED IN CAVES, MUCH
LIKE THE FRENCH ROQUEFORT. GORGONZOLA IS EATEN AS A SOFT CHEESE, BUT IS
ALSO USED IN SAUCES. PECORINO IS THE CLASSIC MOUNTAIN CHEESE, MADE ALL OVER
ITALY, BUT MOST FAMOUSLY IN LAZIO (ROMANO) AND SARDINIA (SARDO). A HARD
CHEESE, IT CAN BE GRATED LIKE PARMESAN. FONTINA IS SEMI-SOFT, MELTS WELL
(IDEAL IN THE PIEDMONTESE FONDUTA), AND IS DELICIOUS, BUT HAS A 45 PER CENT
FAT CONTENT!

formaggi

CHEESE

A LIGHT AND NOURISHING SOUP WHOSE NAME DERIVES FROM THE SOFT FLAKES FORMED BY THE EGG. IT IS ASSOCIATED WITH ROME FOR SOME REASON, BUT IT USES PECORINO MADE IN THE MOUNTAINS. IT'S INCREDIBLY POPULAR WITH CHILDREN BECAUSE OF THE SNOWFLAKE EFFECT, AND IS EATEN THROUGHOUT THE SHORT WINTER MONTHS IN ITALY.

stracciatella

'RAGGED' EGG SOUP

SERVES 6

1 LITRE (1¾ PINTS) VEGETABLE BROTH
   (SEE PAGE 188)

2 LARGE FREE-RANGE EGGS

2 TBSP FINE SEMOLINA

55G (2OZ) PECORINO ROMANO CHEESE,
   FRESHLY GRATED, PLUS EXTRA TO GARNISH

A HANDFUL OF FRESH FLAT-LEAF PARSLEY,
   FINELY CHOPPED

FRESHLY GRATED NUTMEG TO TASTE

SEA SALT AND FRESHLY GROUND BLACK PEPPER

1 Heat all but 3 tbsp of the broth to boiling point.

2 In a bowl, beat together the eggs, semolina, cheese, parsley, nutmeg and the reserved broth.

3 Stirring continuously with a fork, add this to the pan of broth, season to taste and bring just to boiling point.

4 Immediately pour into a warmed tureen or soup bowls. Hand around grated pecorino separately.

IN ITALY, WHEN BROAD BEANS HAVE JUST COME INTO SEASON AND ARE VERY
YOUNG AND TENDER, THEY ARE EATEN RAW. THE LOCALS SIT EATING THE BEANS
AS *PASSA TEMPO*, WITH A GLASS OF CRISP WHITE WINE, TO PASS THE TIME. AT THE
RISTORANTE CAPPUCCINI CONVENT IN AMALFI THEY SERVE THEM COOKED WITH
GOAT'S CHEESE. THIS RECIPE ORIGINATES FROM THERE.

fave con formaggio

BROAD BEANS WITH FRESH CHEESE

SERVES 4

1KG (2¼LB) FRESH BROAD OR BORLOTTI BEANS

4 TBSP OLIVE OIL

2 RED ONIONS (ITALIAN ARE BEST), PEELED AND
   ROUGHLY CHOPPED

SEA SALT AND FRESHLY GROUND BLACK PEPPER

A HANDFUL EACH OF FRESH FLAT-LEAF PARSLEY
   AND MARJORAM, CHOPPED

250G (9OZ) SOFT, BARELY SALTED SHEEP'S
   (A YOUNG PECORINO) OR GOAT'S CHEESE

1   Shell the beans. Heat the olive oil in a saucepan, add the
    onions and fry for 5-10 minutes until golden.

2   Add the beans and stir for 1-2 minutes, then cover with water
    and season with salt and pepper. If using borlotti beans, boil
    for 5 minutes and then simmer for 10 minutes, until the
    beans are very tender and the liquid has evaporated
    completely. If using broad beans, just simmer for 10 minutes
    as above. Mix in the herbs and adjust the seasoning.

3   Cut the cheese into eight thick slices and warm under the
    grill. Serve with the hot beans.

THESE ONIONS COME FROM THE NORTH OF ITALY, FROM PIEDMONT. IN
MOUNTAINOUS AREAS THERE THE PEOPLE ARE FAIRLY FRUGAL OUT OF NECESSITY.
IN ORDER TO MAKE THE MOST OF THEIR LIMITED INGREDIENTS,
THEY HAVE BECOME EXPERT AT PADDING OUT BASICS SUCH AS ONIONS.

cipolle farcite

STUFFED ONIONS

SERVES 4

4 MEDIUM ONIONS

115G (4OZ) PARMESAN CHEESE, FRESHLY
   GRATED

A HANDFUL OF FRESH FLAT-LEAF PARSLEY,
   CHOPPED

2 LARGE FREE-RANGE EGG YOLKS

85G (3OZ) BUTTER AT ROOM TEMPERATURE

SEA SALT AND FRESHLY GROUND BLACK PEPPER

3 TBSP DRY WHITE WINE

1   Peel the onions and top or tail slightly, reserving the lid
    (if preferred, leave the skins on to give the onions a rustic
    look). Cook in boiling water for 15 minutes, then drain.

2   Preheat the oven to 200°C (400°F) gas mark 6.

3   Cut the onions in half widthways then scoop out two-thirds of
    the centres. Chop these and put in a bowl with the Parmesan,
    parsley, egg yolks, 25g (1oz) of the butter, and some salt and
    pepper. Mix thoroughly, then spoon into half the onion shells
    and replace the tops.

4   Melt the remaining butter in a flameproof casserole, put the
    onions in the dish and sprinkle with the wine. Bake in the
    preheated oven for 30-40 minutes, then serve immediately.

THIS IS TYPICAL MOUNTAIN FOOD FROM LOMBARDY. THE RICHNESS OF THE CREAM DIFFUSES THE STRENGTH OF THE CHEESE, WHILE THE FENNEL HAS A GREAT AFFINITY WITH THE CHEESE. POTATOES COULD BE ADDED TO RING THE CHANGES: SLICE THEM AND STEAM WITH THE FENNEL.

crostata di finocchio con aglio e gorgonzola

FENNEL BAKED IN GARLIC AND GORGONZOLA

SERVES 4

2 FENNEL BULBS

1 WHOLE GARLIC BULB

225G (8OZ) GORGONZOLA CHEESE

50ML (2FL OZ) SINGLE CREAM

SEA SALT AND FRESHLY GROUND BLACK PEPPER

115G (4OZ) BREADCRUMBS, TOASTED

BUTTER FOR GREASING

1 Preheat the oven to 200°C (400°F) gas mark 6.

2 Trim the fennel and wash well. Quarter it and cut into even slices, then steam for 8 minutes until tender.

3 Put the whole garlic bulb on a baking tray and bake in the preheated oven for 20 minutes until soft. Remove the papery layers from the bulb, leaving the soft garlic cloves. Pass the cloves through a sieve to obtain a purée.

4 Chop the cheese and put it in a bowl. Add the garlic purée, cream and some salt and pepper, and mix well. Taste and adjust the seasoning if you feel it needs more salt and pepper.

5 Butter an ovenproof serving dish and put in a layer of fennel and then a layer of the cheese mixture. Repeat these layers, then finish with toasted breadcrumbs.

6 Bake in the oven for 20 minutes until crisp and bubbling.

THIS IS ANOTHER 'FRUGAL' MOUNTAIN RECIPE FROM PIEDMONT, USING SIMPLE
CARBOHYDRATE INGREDIENTS IN A DELICIOUSLY CREATIVE WAY. POTATOES, CHEESE,
HERBS AND EGGS ARE COMBINED TO MAKE A WHOLE MUCH MORE INTERESTING
THAN ITS INDIVIDUAL PARTS. YOU COULD USE SALAMI IN THIS AS WELL, OR
PERHAPS INSTEAD OF THE HERBS, AND I HAVE USED DRIED CEPS (PORCINI) IN IT
ON OCCASION TOO.

torta di patate

POTATO TART

SERVES 6

BUTTER FOR GREASING

675G (1LB 7¾OZ) KING EDWARD OR DESIRÉE
  POTATOES, CUT INTO 2.5CM (1IN) CHUNKS

SEA SALT AND FRESHLY GROUND BLACK PEPPER

3 LARGE FREE-RANGE EGGS, BEATEN

2 TBSP ITALIAN '00' PLAIN FLOUR

A HANDFUL EACH OF CHOPPED FRESH CHIVES,
  MINT, PARSLEY AND THYME, PLUS TORN BASIL

30G (1¼OZ) PARMESAN CHEESE, FRESHLY GRATED

125G (4½OZ) PECORINO CHEESE, CUT INTO
  SMALL DICE

85G (3OZ) AGED GORGONZOLA CHEESE, CUT
  INTO SMALL DICE

1 Preheat the oven to 200°C (400°F) gas mark 6, and butter
   a 25cm (10in) pie plate or tart tin.

2 Place the potatoes in a large saucepan, with enough cold
   water to cover them by 5cm (2in). Add salt to taste, then
   bring to the boil. Boil the potatoes, uncovered, for
   15-20 minutes, or until tender when pierced with a knife.
   Drain in a colander.

3 Purée the potatoes through the medium disc of a food mill or
   mouli. Blend with the eggs, flour, herbs, black pepper to taste
   and Parmesan. Fold in the pecorino and Gorgonzola.

4 Spoon the mixture into the pie plate or tart tin and spread
   evenly. Bake for 35-40 minutes or until puffed and golden
   brown. Allow to rest for 5 minutes before serving.

THERE ARE MANY RECIPES FOR THIS CLASSIC DISH, WHICH IS EATEN AND ENJOYED ALL OVER ITALY. THIS IS A REAL FAMILY FAVOURITE OF MINE, AND I TEACH IT IN ITALY A LOT, AS IT IS SO SIMPLE TO MAKE. MANY RECIPES INCLUDE MOZZARELLA, BUT IN THIS PARTICULAR RECIPE THE EGG FORMS THE BINDING.

melanzane alla parmigiana

AUBERGINE, TOMATO AND PARMESAN BAKE

SERVES 6

4 AUBERGINES, CUT INTO 5MM (¼IN) THICK
    SLICES

FINE SALT

1KG (2¼LB) PLUM TOMATOES, ROUGHLY CHOPPED

2 GARLIC CLOVES, PEELED AND CRUSHED

OLIVE OIL

2 TBSP TOMATO PURÉE

100G (3½OZ) PARMESAN CHEESE, FRESHLY GRATED

A HANDFUL OF FRESH BASIL, TORN

SEA SALT AND FRESHLY GROUND BLACK PEPPER

2 LARGE FREE-RANGE EGGS, BEATEN

1   Preheat the oven to 200°C (400°F) gas mark 6. Set a colander over a plate and layer the aubergines in it, sprinkling a little salt between each layer. Set aside for 30 minutes, then rinse and drain. Pat dry with kitchen paper.

2   In a shallow pan, mix together the tomatoes, garlic and 2 tbsp of olive oil. Cover and cook over a medium heat for 3 minutes. Uncover and reduce the heat, stirring constantly for a further 8 minutes. Push the mixture through a sieve and discard the seeds and skin. Stir in the tomato purée.

3   Lightly oil a griddle or frying pan with 2 tbsp of the olive oil. Cook the aubergines over a high heat in batches if necessary, until well browned and cooked (about 5-7 minutes). Use more oil as necessary. Drain on kitchen paper.

4   Place a few aubergine slices in the bottom of an ovenproof dish and spoon over some tomato sauce. Sprinkle with Parmesan and basil leaves. Season, then repeat with the remaining ingredients. Pour the egg over the top, sprinkle over a little more Parmesan and bake for 30 minutes, until golden. Serve at once.

AT FIRST GLANCE YOU MIGHT THINK THESE DUMPLINGS WOULD BE HEAVY AND
ARTERY-CLOGGING, BUT IN REALITY THEY ARE LIGHT, FLUFFY AND DELICIOUS. THE
GORGONZOLA REALLY ENHANCES THE TASTE OF THE RICOTTA. THEY ARE SIMPLE TO
PREPARE AND CAN BE MADE AHEAD OF TIME. SERVE WITH A CRISP GREEN SALAD.

gnocchi di ricotta e salsa di gorgonzola

RICOTTA AND NUTMEG DUMPLINGS WITH GORGONZOLA SAUCE

SERVES 6

400G (14OZ) RICOTTA CHEESE

2 TBSP FRESHLY GRATED PARMESAN CHEESE

3 LARGE FREE-RANGE EGG YOLKS

5 TBSP FINE SEMOLINA

A GOOD PINCH OF FRESHLY GRATED NUTMEG

SEA SALT AND FRESHLY GROUND BLACK PEPPER

1 TBSP CHOPPED FRESH FLAT-LEAF PARSLEY TO
SERVE

GORGONZOLA SAUCE

15G (½OZ) BUTTER

2 TBSP DOUBLE CREAM

115G (4OZ) GORGONZOLA CHEESE, CRUMBLED

1   In a bowl, mash the ricotta with the Parmesan, egg yolks,
semolina, nutmeg, and some salt and pepper to taste.
Mix well together to form a paste.

2   On a lightly oiled surface, roll the paste into thin sausages
about 1cm (½in) in diameter, then cut with a sharp knife into
balls or pieces about 2cm (¾in) long.

3   For the sauce, melt the butter with the cream in a saucepan.
Add the Gorgonzola and cook over a very low heat, crushing
and stirring the cheese until you have a well blended sauce.

4   Bring a large pan of water to the boil and lower the
dumplings in, one at a time, on a slotted spoon. Let them
simmer for about 2 minutes, or until they rise to the surface.
Remove with the slotted spoon and drain thoroughly.

5   Serve the dumplings hot, with the sauce poured over and
sprinkled with parsley.

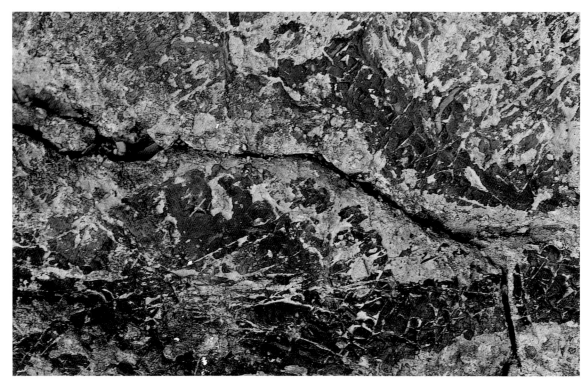

WHEN ON A BOOK-SIGNING AND PUBLICITY TOUR OF AMERICA, I MET THE MOTHER
OF A FRIEND OF MINE IN CHICAGO (BOTH MOTHER AND DAUGHTER ARE FINE
COOKS). I WAS DOING A COOKERY DEMONSTRATION AND, AT THE END OF THE
EVENING, SHE PRESSED THIS RECIPE INTO MY HAND AND URGED ME TO TRY IT.
I DID AND IT'S WONDERFUL. I THANK HER VERY MUCH!

focaccia di gorgonzola

DIANE'S GORGONZOLA BREAD

SERVES ABOUT 8

2 MEDIUM POTATOES, PEELED AND CHOPPED

500-550G (18-20OZ) PLAIN FLOUR

15G (½OZ) FRESH YEAST

250ML (9FL OZ) WARM WATER

2 TBSP OLIVE OIL, PLUS SOME FOR OILING

2 TSP SALT

TOPPING

1 X 400G CAN CHOPPED ITALIAN TOMATOES,
    DRAINED

1 TBSP CHOPPED FRESH OREGANO

2 TBSP TORN FRESH BASIL

1 GARLIC CLOVE, PEELED AND FINELY CHOPPED

½ TSP FRESHLY GROUND BLACK PEPPER

375G (13OZ) QUARTERED ARTICHOKE HEARTS
    MARINATED IN OLIVE OIL

250G (9OZ) GORGONZOLA CHEESE, CRUMBLED

1 MOZZARELLA CHEESE, APPROX. 150G (5½OZ),
    SHREDDED

1 In a covered saucepan, cook the potatoes in a little boiling water for 10-15 minutes, or until tender. Drain and mash, then leave to cool slightly.

2 In a large bowl, stir together two-thirds of the flour and the yeast. Add the water, olive oil and salt. Beat with an electric mixer on medium for 30 seconds, scraping the sides of the bowl, then beat on high for 5 minutes. Stir in the potatoes and as much of the remaining flour as you can with a wooden spoon.

3 On a lightly floured surface, knead in enough of the remaining flour to make a stiff dough that is smooth and elastic (8-10 minutes). Shape the dough into a ball and place in an oiled bowl, turning once to grease the surface. Cover and let rise in a warm place until doubled in size (50-60 minutes).

4 Punch the dough down, cover and let it rest for 10 minutes. Grease a 38 x 25 x 2.5cm (15 x 10 x 1in) baking pan. Press the dough into the pan; if the dough is sticky, sprinkle the surface with about 1 tbsp of flour. Using your fingertips, make small indentations in the dough. Cover and let rise until nearly doubled (about 30 minutes). Meanwhile, preheat the oven to 180°C (350°F) gas mark 4.

5 For the topping, combine the tomatoes, oregano, basil, garlic and pepper, and spoon evenly over the dough. Place the artichoke hearts over the tomato sauce mixture. Cover with the Gorgonzola and shredded mozzarella cheeses. Bake in the preheated oven for 55 minutes. Serve hot.

RICOTTA, A BY-PRODUCT OF PECORINO-MAKING, IS EVER MORE WIDELY USED IN COOKING. IT IS LIGHT, DIGESTIBLE AND INCREDIBLY VERSATILE. IT IS A WONDERFUL CARRIER OF OTHER FLAVOURS – HERE THE ORANGE PEEL, LEMON AND ALMONDS. YOU COULD ADD FURTHER FLAVOUR BY SOAKING THE SULTANAS IN VIN SANTO OR MARSALA. THIS IS THE SORT OF THING ITALIANS MIGHT EAT FOR BREAKFAST!

budino di ricotta

RICOTTA CHEESECAKE

SERVES 6

A LITTLE BUTTER FOR GREASING

40G (1½OZ) DRY WHITE BREADCRUMBS

225G (8OZ) RICOTTA CHEESE

40G (1½OZ) CANDIED ORANGE PEEL,
   FINELY CHOPPED

3 LARGE FREE-RANGE EGG YOLKS

85G (3OZ) CASTER SUGAR

55G (2OZ) GROUND ALMONDS

40G (1½OZ) SULTANAS

FINELY GRATED ZEST OF 1 UNWAXED LEMON

A LITTLE ICING SUGAR FOR DUSTING

1   Preheat the oven to 180°C (350°F) gas mark 4. Butter a 15cm (6in) diameter springform cake tin and coat with three-quarters of the breadcrumbs.

2   Mix the ricotta and orange peel in a mixing bowl. Beat the egg yolks and sugar together until light and fluffy. Add the cheese and peel mixture, almonds, sultanas and lemon zest.

3   Transfer to the prepared tin, smooth the surface and sprinkle with the remaining breadcrumbs. Cook in the centre of the preheated oven for about 30 minutes.

4   Remove from the oven and leave until quite cold. Remove from the tin and dust with icing sugar.

'HARDY' HERBS GROW HIGHER UP, OR IN COOLER TEMPERATURES, THAN 'SOFT' HERBS (SEE PAGE 152). HERBS CONTAIN AROMATIC ESSENTIAL OILS IN THEIR LEAVES, AND IN HARDY HERBS THESE OILS ARE LESS VOLATILE THAN IN SOFTER HERBS BECAUSE OF THE CLIMATE EXTREMES TO WHICH THEY HAVE BEEN EXPOSED. FOR INSTANCE, YOU COULD HAPPILY ADD A BAY LEAF OR A SPRIG OF FRESH THYME OR ROSEMARY TO A STEW; A SPRIG OF BASIL WOULD LOSE ITS UNIQUE FRAGRANCE VERY SWIFTLY ON BEING COOKED.

HARDY HERBS ARE USED A LOT IN ITALIAN COOKING, PARTICULARLY BAY, THYME, ROSEMARY AND SAGE. BAY IS USED IN *AROMI*, THE ITALIAN EQUIVALENT OF A BOUQUET GARNI, AND IN MARINADES. THYME GROWS WILD ALL OVER THE MEDITERRANEAN MOUNTAINS, AND IS USED IN MANY MEAT DISHES, IN *AROMI*, AND IN MARINADES FOR OLIVES. ROSEMARY GOES WELL WITH ROASTED MEATS, AND IS USED ALL OVER THE COUNTRY TO SCENT FOCACCIA. SAGE IS ONE OF THE MOST POPULAR HARDY HERBS, AND IS USED WITH WHITE MEATS (ESPECIALLY PORK, A TUSCAN SPECIALITY) AND CALVES' LIVER AND IN STUFFED PASTAS.

erbe robuste

HARDY HERBS

SOME OF ITALY'S BEST HAZELNUTS COME FROM PIEDMONT, AND THEY TASTE
WONDERFUL WITH WILD MOUNTAIN SAGE. I FIRST ENCOUNTERED THIS FOCACCIA
IN LIGURIA, A REGION FAMOUS FOR ITS HERBS. THERE A LITTLE BAKERY MADE
HUGE SHEETS OF THIS BREAD, AND I DISCOVERED THAT THEY PUT WINE IN THEIR
DOUGH. THIS MAKES THE YEAST LIGHTER, ALMOST LIKE AN EXTRA FERMENTATION.

focaccia di salvia e nocciole

SAGE AND HAZELNUT FOCACCIA

SERVES ABOUT 6

BIGA

2.5G (⅛OZ) FRESH YEAST

150ML (5FL OZ) WARM WATER, AT BLOOD
     TEMPERATURE

125G (4½OZ) STRONG WHITE FLOUR

DOUGH

10G (⅓OZ) FRESH YEAST

85ML (3FL OZ) WARM WATER, AT BLOOD
     TEMPERATURE

1½ TSP SALT

375G (13OZ) STRONG WHITE FLOUR

20 FRESH SAGE LEAVES, CHOPPED

3 TBSP OLIVE OIL

85ML (3FL OZ) WHITE WINE

TOPPING

OLIVE OIL

SEA SALT

ABOUT 10 FRESH SAGE LEAVES, TORN

150G (5½OZ) SKINNED HAZELNUTS, TOASTED

1 To make the biga, dissolve the fresh yeast in the warm water. Add the flour and mix to a smooth, thick batter. Cover and leave to ferment at room temperature for 12-36 hours, until loose and bubbling.

2 To make the dough, dissolve the fresh yeast in the water. In a large bowl, mix the salt into the flour. Make a well in the centre. Add the chopped sage leaves and pour in the yeast mixture, olive oil and biga, and combine them together. Add the wine and mix to form a soft, sticky dough, adding extra water if necessary.

3 Turn out on to a floured surface and knead until smooth, silky and elastic (about 10 minutes). Place the dough in a clean oiled bowl, cover and leave to rise until doubled in size (about 1½-2 hours).

4 Knock back and chafe (a rotating, shaping motion), then rest for 10 minutes. Roll out to approximately 1cm (½in) in thickness. Place on an oiled baking sheet, cover and prove until doubled in size (about 60 minutes).

5 Meanwhile, preheat the oven to 200°C (400°F) gas mark 6.

6 Press on the top of the dough with your fingers to form dimples. Sprinkle with olive oil, sea salt, fresh sage leaves and toasted hazelnuts. Bake in the preheated oven for 30 minutes, or until golden brown and hollow sounding when tapped on the base. Remove from the oven and sprinkle with extra olive oil.

THE PUNGENCY OF THE SAGE IS A GREAT FLAVOUR ENHANCER FOR THE FAIRLY BLAND PUMPKIN HERE. CHOOSING THE RIGHT PUMPKIN IS VITAL. IT SHOULD NOT BE TOO LARGE, NOR TOO SMALL; TAP IT, AND IT SHOULD FEEL TIGHT AS A DRUM, HEAVY FOR ITS SIZE. IF IT'S LIGHT, THE CHANCES ARE IT'S OLD. YOU'LL NEED AT LEAST A 1KG (2¼LB) PUMPKIN TO GET THIS AMOUNT OF FLESH AFTER PEELING AND SEEDING. KEEP THE SEEDS AS A COOK'S TREAT: WASH, DRY AND BAKE WITH SEA SALT.

zucca fritta con salvia e parmigiano

PUMPKIN FRITTERS WITH SAGE AND PARMESAN

SERVES 4

750G (1LB 10OZ) PUMPKIN FLESH

200G (7OZ) ITALIAN '00' PLAIN FLOUR

A HANDFUL OF FRESH SAGE, FINELY CHOPPED,
    PLUS EXTRA TO GARNISH

115G (4OZ) PARMESAN CHEESE, FRESHLY GRATED

SEA SALT AND FRESHLY GROUND BLACK PEPPER

2 GARLIC CLOVES, PEELED AND FINELY CHOPPED

4 TBSP OLIVE OIL

1   Chop the pumpkin flesh into even cubes.

2   Put the flesh into boiling salted water and cook for about 8 minutes, until tender. Drain and mash in a bowl. Add the flour, sage, half of the Parmesan, some salt and pepper and the garlic, and knead until smooth.

3   Form into a long sausage and chop into 12 even pieces. Flatten each piece to form a fritter.

4   Heat the oil in a frying pan and fry the fritters for 3-4 minutes on both sides, until golden. Drain well.

5   Serve sprinkled with the remaining Parmesan and some extra torn sage leaves.

I FOUND THIS RECIPE WHEN I WAS ON A FOOD-TASTING TRIP IN LIGURIA AND,
OF THE MANY OLIVE BREADS WE TRIED, THIS WAS OUR FAVOURITE – PROBABLY
BECAUSE OF THE WONDERFUL FLAVOUR OF THE LIGURIAN THYME. DO USE THE
BEST OLIVES YOU CAN FIND, PREFERABLY THOSE YOU HAVE MARINATED YOURSELF
(SEE PAGE 22). THE BOTTLED WATER MAY SEEM ODD HERE, BUT IT REALLY DOES
IMPROVE THE FLAVOUR.

pane con timo e olive

THYME AND OLIVE BREAD

MAKES 4 SMALL LOAVES

15G (½OZ) FRESH YEAST

200-250ML (7-9FL OZ) BOTTLED WATER,
    HAND-HOT

450G (1LB) STRONG WHITE ORGANIC FLOUR

½ TSP SEA SALT

3 TBSP OLIVE OIL

150G (5½OZ) BLACK OLIVES, STONED AND
    CHOPPED

6 SPRIGS FRESH THYME, LEAVES STRIPPED
    FROM THE STALKS

1 Mix the yeast and 50ml (2fl oz) of the water. Cover and
   leave to froth for 15 minutes.

2 Put the flour and salt in a bowl together with the olive oil.
   Pour the frothy yeast into the flour along with most of the
   remaining water and work it into a stiff, sticky dough. Add
   the remaining water.

3 Knead for 10 minutes, until smooth and elastic. Add the
   olives and thyme leaves and knead into the dough.

4 Cover the bowl with a damp cloth and leave the dough
   in a warm place to rise for 1½ hours.

5 Knead the dough again for a few minutes, then divide into
   four balls. Place the balls on an oiled baking tray. Press
   down gently and shape any way you like. Let the dough
   rise again, covered, for about half an hour.

6 Preheat the oven to 200°C (400°F) gas mark 6.

7 Brush the loaves with water to soften the crust and
   bake for 30 minutes. Cool on a wire rack.

foreste e boschi
forests and woods

YOU CAN SEE FORESTS OF MAGNIFICENT TREES ALL OVER ITALY, FROM THE FOOTHILLS OF THE ALPS RIGHT DOWN TO THE BLEAK, RUGGEDLY BEAUTIFUL LANDSCAPE OF CALABRIA. IN SOME SENSES, AND CERTAINLY TO ME, ITALY IS DEFINED BY HER TREES, FROM THE MAGNIFICENT CHESTNUTS AND OAKS OF DECIDUOUS FORESTS TO THE EVERGREEN UMBRELLA PINES THAT RISE LIKE BLACK COLUMNS FROM THE SUN-BAKED EARTH ALONG THE TUSCAN COASTLINES.

FORESTS AND WOODS ARE USUALLY THOUGHT OF AS QUIET, PEACEFUL, SERENE PLACES, BUT IN ITALY THEY ARE HIVES OF ACTIVITY, WITH THE ITALIANS PICKING AND GATHERING NUTS, MUSHROOMS AND FRUITS ALMOST ALL YEAR ROUND. THESE ARE THE HOMES OF THE WILD FUNGI ABOUT WHICH THE ITALIANS ARE SO VERY PASSIONATE. THE FIRST FUNGI FORAY OF THE YEAR IS OFTEN IN SEARCH OF MORELS, BETWEEN THE MONTHS OF MARCH AND MAY. THEN, FROM EARLY SUMMER, THE HUNT BEGINS FOR THE HIGHLY-PRIZED CAESAR'S MUSHROOMS (OR *OVOLI* OR CHANTERELLES). THIS TOO IS THE TIME FOR THE WONDERFUL CEPS (OR PORCINI) – THESE ARE EATEN EITHER RAW OR COOKED AND THEY ARE DRIED FOR USE IN KITCHENS THROUGHOUT THE YEAR, AS NO ITALIAN LARDER COULD BE WITHOUT THIS MAGNIFICENTLY FLAVOURSOME INGREDIENT. YOU CAN FREQUENTLY SEE HUGE BOXES OF CEPS FOR SALE ALONG MOST OF ITALY'S MINOR ROADS THROUGHOUT THE SEASON.

ITALIANS LOVE TO DRESS UP WHEN HUNTING FOR MUSHROOMS, AND AFTER A SUCCESSFUL TRIP THEY OFTEN GATHER IN GROUPS, COOKING THEIR TREASURES (USUALLY WITH GARLIC AND PARSLEY) OVER AN OPEN FIRE, YET STILL ALLOWING THEMSELVES PLENTY TO KEEP.

HOWEVER, THE BIGGEST PRIZE OF ALL IS THE TRUFFLE. THE WHITE TRUFFLE IS CONSIDERED TO BE THE BEST, AND THIS GROWS IN SYMBIOSIS WITH OAK, HAZEL, POPLAR AND BEECH TREES, ALMOST EXCLUSIVELY

IN PIEDMONT (ALTHOUGH IT CAN BE FOUND IN THE MARCHES AS WELL). BLACK TRUFFLES ARE A SPECIALITY OF THE UMBRIAN FORESTS, AND I REMEMBER SEARCHING AMONG THE OAK TREES WHILE ON A TRUFFLE HUNT THERE, FOLLOWING A SMALL, EXPERT DOG. WE WERE FORTUNATE ENOUGH TO FIND A TRUFFLE! OUR GUIDE WAS VERY CLOAK-AND-DAGGER, HIDING THE VAN IN THE BUSHES AND POURING HIS HOME-MADE WINE DOWN OUR THROATS.I SUPPOSE HE HOPED WE MIGHT BE SO DRUNK THAT WE WOULDN'T BE ABLE TO RETRACE OUR STEPS TO HIS FAVOURITE TRUFFLE LOCATIONS!

NUT TREES FORM A MAJOR PROPORTION OF ITALY'S FORESTS. CHESTNUT TREES IN PARTICULAR ARE TO BE FOUND EVERYWHERE — SOME CULTIVATED, SOME WILD. MANY A FOREST-WALKER WILL COLLECT A BAGFUL OF CHESTNUTS TO TAKE HOME TO ROAST OR BOIL, AND THEY ARE A STAPLE OF TUSCAN COOKING. ALL OVER ITALY, HAZELNUTS, WALNUTS, ALMONDS AND PINE NUTS ARE USED EXTENSIVELY IN COOKING AND ARE MADE INTO LIQUEURS: PINE NUTS FEATURE IN THE FAMOUS GENOESE PESTO (ALTHOUGH WALNUTS ARE SOMETIMES USED INSTEAD); THE LIGURIAN FILLED PASTA, *PANSÔTI*, IS ALWAYS SERVED WITH A WALNUT SAUCE; AND BOTH WALNUTS AND HAZELNUTS ARE USED IN MANY OF THE SWEET DISHES OF THE NORTH — THE CAKES, TARTS, NOUGAT AND ICE-CREAMS. THE WONDERFUL OILS EXPRESSED FROM THESE NUTS ARE ALSO OFTEN USED IN ITALIAN COOKING.

FESTIVALS ARE HELD ALL OVER ITALY TO CELEBRATE THE AUTUMN NUT (AND OLIVE) CROP. ONE OF THE MOST FAMOUS OF THESE FESTIVALS IS THE *FESTA DEL MANDORLATO* (ALMONDS) IN VERONA. ALMONDS ARE ALSO GROUND AND BAKED IN BISCUITS (THE AMARETTI OF MODENA ARE ALMOST AS RENOWNED AS THE TOWN'S BALSAMIC VINEGAR), AND ALMOND BLOSSOMS PERFUME THE AIR, ESPECIALLY IN THE EXTENSIVE ALMOND GROVES OF PUGLIA.

WHEN THE AUTUMN MISTS FILL ITALY'S WOODS AND FORESTS, SO TOO DOES THE FRAGRANCE OF WILD FUNGI – MUSHROOMS SUCH AS CEPS (PORCINI), CHANTERELLES, CAESAR'S MUSHROOMS AND THE UNDISPUTED KING OF FUNGI, THE TRUFFLE. THE WOODS FILL TOO WITH WALKERS, BASKETS AT THE READY FOR COLLECTING FUNGAL BOOTY. ONCE THESE ADVENTUROUS FORAGERS HAVE GOT THEIR MUSHROOMS HOME, THEY WILL PROBABLY DRY THEM IN THE AUTUMN SUN (OR IN A LOW OVEN), TO BE USED THROUGHOUT THE WINTER TO ENHANCE THE FLAVOUR OF RISOTTOS, CASSEROLES AND PASTA DISHES. TRUFFLES ARE EVEN MORE REVERED THAN MOST FUNGI, AND VIRTUAL WARS HAVE BROKEN OUT BETWEEN RIVALS FOR THE SAME RICH TRUFFLING SPOTS. TRUFFLES USED TO BE SOUGHT OUT BY PIGS BUT, AS THESE PIGS PROVED THEMSELVES TO BE CLASSICALLY GREEDY, SMALL, HIGHLY INTELLIGENT DOGS ARE USED NOW INSTEAD (THEY GET REWARDED WITH A BISCUIT; MUCH CHEAPER!).

IF YOU BUY DRIED MUSHROOMS (USUALLY CEPS), CHOOSE THOSE THAT ARE LIGHT IN COLOUR, AS THE DARKER THEY ARE THE OLDER THEY ARE. BIG PIECES ARE BEST. TRY TO KEEP DRIED MUSHROOMS IN THE FRIDGE.

funghi

FUNGI

THIS IS A RISOTTO OF PURE INDULGENCE, THANKS TO THE WHITE TRUFFLE. THE *SOFFRITTO* BASE IS ONE OF THE MOST ESSENTIAL ITALIAN FLAVOURINGS – FRIED ONION OR SHALLOT, USUALLY COMBINED WITH OTHER VEGETABLES SUCH AS CARROT. WE KEEP IT IN JARS IN THE FRIDGE, READY FOR STARTING OFF A SOUP OR RISOTTO (IT KEEPS WELL FOR UP TO FOUR DAYS).

risotto al tartufo bianco

WHITE TRUFFLE RISOTTO

SERVES 4

900ML (32FL OZ) VEGETABLE BROTH
   (SEE PAGE 188)
55G (2OZ) UNSALTED BUTTER
1 TBSP OLIVE OIL
8 SHALLOTS, PEELED AND FINELY CHOPPED
275G (10OZ) RISOTTO RICE, SUCH AS
   VIALONE NANO
75ML (2½FL OZ) DRY WHITE WINE
SEA SALT AND FRESHLY GROUND BLACK PEPPER
2 TBSP SINGLE CREAM
115G (4OZ) PARMESAN CHEESE,
   FRESHLY GRATED
2 TBSP TRUFFLE OIL
A HANDFUL OF FRESH FLAT-LEAF PARSLEY,
   ROUGHLY CHOPPED
1 FRESH MEDIUM WHITE TRUFFLE,
   SHAVED PAPER-THIN

1 Bring the broth to a steady simmer in a large saucepan.

2 Heat the butter and olive oil in a sauté pan or a heavy-based casserole over a moderate heat. Add the shallots and sauté for 1-2 minutes, until they begin to soften. Do not brown them.

3 Now add the rice to this *soffritto*. Using a wooden spoon, stir for 1 minute, making sure all the grains are well coated. Add the wine and stir until it is completely absorbed. Begin to add the simmering broth, ladle by ladle, stirring continuously. Wait until each addition is almost absorbed before adding more broth. Reserve a generous ladleful of broth to add at the end.

4 After approximately 18 minutes, when the rice is tender but still firm (*al dente*), add the reserved broth, salt, pepper, cream, Parmesan, truffle oil and parsley. Stir vigorously to combine. Remove from the heat, place the lid on the pan and let the risotto stand for 2 minutes.

5 Garnish each serving with truffle shavings. Serve immediately, on warmed plates.

MUSHROOMS, PARSLEY AND MINT MAKE A CLASSIC UMBRIAN COMBINATION. IF YOU HAVE BEEN OUT ON A WILD MUSHROOM FORAY, YOU COULD BAKE A SELECTION OF MUSHROOMS ALL IN ONE GO. INSTEAD OF WRAPPING THE INGREDIENTS IN PAPER, YOU COULD ENCASE THEM IN FOIL AND COOK THEM ON THE BARBECUE. BOTH VERSIONS PRESERVE THE JUICES – '*IN UMIDO*' – AND THEREFORE THE FLAVOUR.

funghi al cartoccio

BAKED MUSHROOMS

SERVES 4

500G (1LB 2OZ) FIELD MUSHROOMS (OR WILD),
   CLEANED
15G (½OZ) UNSALTED BUTTER, MELTED
4 GARLIC CLOVES, PEELED AND FINELY CHOPPED
A HANDFUL EACH OF FRESH FLAT-LEAF PARSLEY
   AND MINT, FINELY CHOPPED
SEA SALT AND FRESHLY GROUND BLACK PEPPER
4 TBSP OLIVE OIL

1   Preheat the oven to 200°C (400°F) gas mark 6.

2   Wipe the mushrooms with a clean damp cloth and roughly chop.

3   Brush four squares of parchment paper liberally with the butter. Place some of the mushrooms in each square of paper. Sprinkle with garlic, herbs, salt and pepper and olive oil.

4   Bring the corners of each square up to meet in the centre and fold over to seal the contents perfectly.

5   Bake in the preheated oven for 10-15 minutes. Serve wrapped in the paper – slash open and let the smell hit your nose.

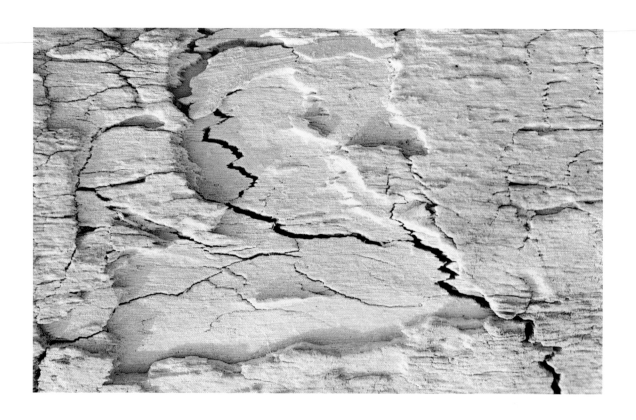

IT'S AN ODD IDEA, THIS SAVOURY CAKE, BUT IT WORKS WELL AND IS VERY TASTY. YOU COULD USE FRESH MUSHROOMS INSTEAD OF THE CEPS, OR A COMBINATION OF FRESH AND DRIED (EVERY ITALIAN LARDER WILL CONTAIN SOME DRIED CEPS OR PORCINI). WE OFTEN INCLUDE THIS LIGURIAN SPECIALITY FROM GENOA IN OUR PICNIC ON THE DAY AFTER EASTER MONDAY.

polpettone di funghi e fagiolini

MUSHROOM AND BEAN SOUFFLÉ CAKE

SERVES 6

55G (2OZ) DRIED CEPS (PORCINI)

450G (1LB) GREEN BEANS (FRENCH)

SEA SALT AND FRESHLY GROUND BLACK PEPPER

55G (2OZ) CRUSTLESS WHITE COUNTRY-TYPE
    BREAD

100ML (3½FL OZ) WHOLE MILK

5 TBSP OLIVE OIL

2 GARLIC CLOVES, PEELED AND VERY FINELY
    CHOPPED

1 TBSP CHOPPED FRESH MARJORAM

A HANDFUL OF FRESH FLAT-LEAF PARSLEY,
    CHOPPED

3 LARGE FREE-RANGE EGGS

25G (1OZ) RICOTTA CHEESE

4 TBSP MASCARPONE CHEESE

55G (2OZ) PARMESAN CHEESE, FRESHLY GRATED

40G (1½OZ) DRIED WHITE BREADCRUMBS,
    PLUS MORE FOR THE TIN

1 Soak the dried ceps in cold water for 15 minutes. Dry them with kitchen paper and chop them coarsely.

2 Top and tail the beans and wash them. Plunge them into plenty of boiling salted water and cook them for just over 5 minutes. Drain and refresh them under cold water and drain thoroughly. Now chop them coarsely by hand.

3 Put the bread in a bowl, add the milk and leave to soak.

4 Preheat the oven to 180°C (350°F) gas mark 4.

5 Heat half the olive oil, the garlic, marjoram and parsley in a frying pan. Add the dried ceps and beans and sauté gently for 2-3 minutes. Squeeze the excess milk out of the bread, and add the bread to the bean mixture, crumbling it through your fingers. Continue to fry for 5 minutes.

6 Beat the eggs together lightly in a large bowl. Crumble in the ricotta, then add the mascarpone, Parmesan, dried breadcrumbs and some salt and pepper. Now add all the contents of the frying pan to the cheese bowl and mix thoroughly. Taste and check the seasoning.

7 Grease a 20 cm (8in) springform cake tin with a little of the remaining olive oil. Sprinkle with enough breadcrumbs to cover the surface. Spoon the bean mixture into the prepared tin and pour over the remaining olive oil in a thin stream. Bake in the preheated oven for about 40 minutes. Let it cool in the tin. Serve hot, warm or cold.

NOT ONE OF ITALY'S GREAT NUT TREES IS ORIGINALLY NATIVE TO THE COUNTRY, BUT
WALNUTS, ALMONDS, HAZELNUTS AND CHESTNUTS HAVE BECOME IMPORTANT FACETS
OF ITALIAN COOKING. THE CHESTNUT HAS BECOME A STAPLE FOOD: IN PIEDMONT AND
TUSCANY IT IS EATEN AS A VEGETABLE, ADDED TO SOUPS AND STEWS OR GROUND TO
MAKE FLOUR AND A FORM OF POLENTA. IT MUST BE COOKED TO BE EDIBLE.

ALMONDS, GROWN MOSTLY IN PUGLIA AND SICILY, LEND TEXTURE AND FLAVOUR
TO BISCUITS, INCLUDING MACAROONS, AND TO CAKES AND MARZIPAN. THEY ALSO
FEATURE IN NOUGATS. HOWEVER, ALMONDS CAN WORK WELL IN SAVOURY DISHES,
THANKS TO AN ARABIC INFLUENCE. WALNUTS ARE MAINLY CULTIVATED IN CAMPANIA
AND THE SOUTH BUT, ODDLY, ARE MOSTLY USED IN THE NORTH. IN LIGURIA A WALNUT
SAUCE IS USED TO DRESS A STUFFED PASTA AND WALNUTS ARE OFTEN SUBSTITUTED
FOR PINE KERNELS IN PESTO. WALNUT TARTS ARE MADE IN MOST ITALIAN REGIONS.
HAZELNUTS ARE USED TO GARNISH CAKES AND TARTS, OR GROUND FOR NOUGAT,
CAKES AND BISCUITS. THEY ARE ALSO USED WHOLE IN *CROCCANTE*, A NUTTY SWEET,
AS ARE ALMONDS.

noci

NUTS

CAMPANIA IS FAMOUS FOR ITS AUBERGINES, LEMONS, SEAFOOD AND ALMONDS. THERE ARE TWO AUBERGINE CROPS A YEAR, THANKS TO THE CLIMATE, WHILE THE LEMONS ARE THE JUICIEST ANYWHERE AND THE ALMOND TREES – SOME OF THEM WILD, SOME CULTIVATED – STRETCH FOR MILES. AT HOME WE ENJOY THIS RECIPE COLD AS AN *ANTIPASTO*, DRIZZLED WITH EXTRA VIRGIN OLIVE OIL.

melanzane farcite

STUFFED AUBERGINE WITH ALMONDS

SERVES 6

3 SMALL AUBERGINES, EACH WEIGHING ABOUT
    225G (8OZ)

6 RIPE PLUM TOMATOES

50ML (2FL OZ) OLIVE OIL

1 ONION, PEELED AND CHOPPED

3 GARLIC CLOVES, PEELED AND CRUSHED

A HANDFUL OF FRESH FLAT-LEAF PARSLEY,
    FINELY CHOPPED

A HANDFUL OF FRESH OREGANO, CHOPPED

55G (2OZ) GROUND ALMONDS

55G (2OZ) BREADCRUMBS

SEA SALT AND FRESHLY GROUND BLACK PEPPER

75G (2¾OZ) PARMESAN CHEESE, FRESHLY GRATED

55G (2OZ) SLIVERED ALMONDS

1   Put the aubergines in a saucepan of boiling water. Cover and simmer for 10 minutes. Remove and halve lengthways. Scoop out the flesh, taking care not to damage the skin, leaving a shell 3mm (⅛in) thick. Roughly chop the flesh.

2   Put the tomatoes in a bowl, cover with boiling water for 30 seconds, then plunge into cold water. Using a sharp knife, peel off the skin, then chop the flesh, discarding the seeds.

3   Preheat the oven to 180°C (350°F) gas mark 4.

4   Heat the olive oil in a frying pan. Add the onion and cook to soften, then add the garlic, parsley and oregano and cook for 3 minutes more. Add the chopped aubergine and tomatoes. Cover and simmer for 10 minutes.

5   Remove the pan from the heat and stir in the ground almonds and breadcrumbs. Season with salt and pepper. Fill the aubergine shells with the mixture and sprinkle with Parmesan.

6   Place the aubergines side-by-side in a well-greased shallow baking dish and bake in the preheated oven for 30 minutes or until the tops brown. Halfway through, sprinkle with the slivered almonds. Serve hot or cold.

THIS IS A NORTHERN RECIPE, USING THE AOSTA VALLEY'S FONTINA CHEESE,
WHOSE WONDERFULLY NUTTY FLAVOUR BLENDS BEAUTIFULLY WITH THE WALNUTS.
THIS IS A GOOD STORE-CUPBOARD RISOTTO. KEEP SHELLED WALNUTS IN THE
FRIDGE AS THEY SOON BECOME RANCID; BUY THEM IN THE SHELL WHEN FRESH
(IN THE AUTUMN) AND USE QUICKLY.

risotto con fontina e noci

WALNUT AND FONTINA RISOTTO

SERVES 6

900ML (32FL OZ) VEGETABLE BROTH
   (SEE PAGE 188)
55G (2OZ) UNSALTED BUTTER
1 TBSP OLIVE OIL
8 SHALLOTS, PEELED AND FINELY CHOPPED
1 GARLIC CLOVE, PEELED AND CRUSHED
275G (9½OZ) RISOTTO RICE, SUCH AS
   VIALONE NANO, CARNAROLI OR ARBORIO
75ML (2½FL OZ) WHITE WINE
100G (3½OZ) FONTINA CHEESE,
   CUT INTO CUBES
100G (3½OZ) PARMESAN CHEESE,
   FRESHLY GRATED
55G (2OZ) SHELLED WALNUTS,
   COARSELY CHOPPED
A HANDFUL OF FRESH FLAT-LEAF PARSLEY,
   COARSELY CHOPPED
SEA SALT AND FRESHLY GROUND BLACK PEPPER
TO SERVE (OPTIONAL)
SHELLED WALNUTS, COARSELY CHOPPED
FRESHLY GRATED PARMESAN CHEESE

1   Put the broth in a saucepan. Heat until almost boiling and then reduce the heat until barely simmering to keep it hot.

2   Heat the butter and olive oil in a sauté pan or heavy-based casserole over a medium heat. Add the shallots and cook for 1-2 minutes, until softened but not browned. Add the garlic and mix well.

3   Add the rice and stir, using a wooden spoon, until the grains are well coated and glistening (about 1 minute). Pour in the wine and stir until it has been absorbed.

4   Add a ladleful of hot broth and simmer, stirring, until it has been absorbed. Continue to add the broth at intervals and cook as before, until the liquid has been absorbed and the rice is tender but still firm (*al dente*) – about 18-20 minutes. Reserve the last ladleful of broth.

5   Add the reserved broth, fontina, Parmesan, walnuts, parsley and some salt and pepper. Stir well. Remove from the heat, cover and allow to rest for 2 minutes.

6   Spoon into warmed bowls, sprinkle with walnuts and grated Parmesan if using, and serve immediately.

MY GRANDMOTHER WAS BORN AND BROUGHT UP IN A SMALL VILLAGE,
MINORI, IN CAMPANIA, AND THIS IS ONE OF HER RECIPES. THE BISCUITS ARE
REALLY MELT-IN-THE-MOUTH, MORE CRUMBLY THAN MACAROONS (BECAUSE OF
THE EQUAL QUANTITIES OF NUTS TO BUTTER). EAT WITH COFFEE OR ICE-CREAM,
OR AS A LITTLE *MERENDA* OR SNACK IN THE AFTERNOON.

biscottini alla mandorla

ALMOND BISCUITS

MAKES ABOUT 16 BISCUITS

125G (4½OZ) SKINNED ALMONDS (OR HAZELNUTS
    ARE WONDERFUL)

125G (4½OZ) UNSALTED BUTTER AT ROOM
    TEMPERATURE, PLUS EXTRA FOR GREASING

1 TSP PURE VANILLA EXTRACT

A PINCH OF SALT

125G (4½OZ) CASTER SUGAR, PLUS A LITTLE
    EXTRA FOR SPRINKLING

125G (4½OZ) ITALIAN '00' PLAIN FLOUR OR
    PLAIN FLOUR

1   Preheat the oven to 180°C (350°F) gas mark 4.

2   Spread the almonds on a baking tray and cook for 4-5 minutes
    in the preheated oven until lightly toasted. Leave to cool, then
    grind in a processor before adding the butter, vanilla and salt.

3   When the mixture is well blended, beat in the sugar. Tip the
    mixture into a bowl, sift in the flour and fold in thoroughly
    to make a dough.

4   Put the bowl in the fridge to chill the dough for about
    1 hour or longer if you wish. Preheat the oven to the same
    temperature as above.

5   Break off pieces of dough about the size of a walnut and roll
    into balls. Press them into 5cm (2in) rounds and place on a
    buttered baking tray about 2cm (¾in) apart. Sprinkle with the
    extra sugar and bake for 8-10 minutes, or until golden. Leave
    to cool on the tray.

THE INCLUSION OF GROUND ALMONDS AND LEMON JUICE MAKES THIS THIN CAKE
WONDERFULLY MOIST. I'VE OFTEN MADE IT AS THE FINAL COURSE FOR SUNDAY
LUNCHES. EVEN AFTER FIVE OTHER COURSES, THIS CAKE GOES DOWN WELL.
I SERVE IT WITH A LEMON-FLAVOURED MASCARPONE.

torta al limone, mandorle e pere

LEMON, ALMOND AND PEAR CAKE

MAKES 1 X 20CM (8IN) CAKE

250G (9OZ) UNSALTED BUTTER, SOFTENED

250G (9OZ) GOLDEN CASTER SUGAR

4 LARGE FREE-RANGE EGGS

55G (2OZ) PLAIN FLOUR, SIFTED

250G (9OZ) GROUND ALMONDS

FINELY GRATED ZEST AND JUICE OF
    2 UNWAXED LEMONS

4 RIPE WILLIAM PEARS, PEELED, HALVED
    AND CORED

ICING SUGAR FOR DUSTING

1 Preheat the oven to 180°C (350°F) gas mark 4. Line the base of a 20cm (8in) diameter springform cake tin with parchment paper.

2 Cream together the butter and sugar in a bowl until soft. Beat in the eggs, one at a time, adding some flour after each addition, until all the eggs and flour have been included.

3 Fold in the almonds and the lemon zest and juice. Spoon the mixture into the prepared cake tin and smooth over.

4 Make six cuts lengthways in each pear half without cutting all the way through at one end. Top the mixture in the tin with the pears, fanned-out. Bake in the preheated oven for 1 hour, or until a skewer comes out clean. If the cake is browning too quickly cover with a piece of foil.

5 Cool and dust with icing sugar to serve.

THERE ARE MANY VARIATIONS OF *PANFORTE*, BUT THIS
IS MY TAKE ON IT. IT INCLUDES SOME FAIRLY UNUSUAL
INGREDIENTS, IN PARTICULAR THE CANDIED PINEAPPLE AND
GROUND CORIANDER. *PANFORTE* USED TO BE EATEN BY THE
ITALIAN CRUSADERS FOR STRENGTH AND ENERGY DURING THE
WARS, AND IT'S THE SORT OF THING YOU WOULD TAKE WITH
YOU NOW WHEN LONG-DISTANCE WALKING. THROUGHOUT
TUSCANY YOU CAN SEE LARGE SLABS OF PANFORTE ON
DISPLAY, SOME THICK, SOME THIN, BUT ALL PACKED WITH
NUTS, FRUIT AND HONEY – INSTANT ENERGY!

panforte

NOUGAT

SERVES 8-16

115G (4OZ) HAZELNUTS

115G (4OZ) WHOLE BLANCHED ALMONDS

35G (1¼OZ) CANDIED PINEAPPLE, CHOPPED

35G (1¼OZ) EACH OF CANDIED APRICOTS
   AND CANDIED GINGER, IN 5MM (¼IN) SLICES

35G (1¼OZ) DRIED FIGS, STEMS REMOVED,
   THEN CUT INTO SMALL PIECES

125G (4½OZ) MIXED PEEL, FINELY CHOPPED

1 TSP GROUND CINNAMON

½ TSP EACH OF GROUND CORIANDER,
   GROUND CLOVES AND FRESHLY
   GRATED NUTMEG

3 PINCHES FRESHLY GROUND BLACK PEPPER

90G (3¼OZ) STRONG FLOUR OR ITALIAN
   '00' FLOUR

150G (5½OZ) GRANULATED SUGAR

125G (4½OZ) FRAGRANT HONEY

35G (1¼OZ) UNSALTED BUTTER

ICING SUGAR TO DUST

1   Preheat the oven to 180°C (350°F) gas mark 4.

2   Line a 20cm (8in) diameter springform cake tin with
parchment paper.

3   To roast the hazelnuts, place on a baking tray and put into the
preheated oven for 10-15 minutes. Rub the skins from the
hazelnuts in a clean tea-towel. Roast the blanched almonds for
10-15 minutes, until they turn a very pale golden colour.
Once cool, coarsely chop the hazelnuts and almonds. Reduce
the oven temperature to 150°C (300°F) gas mark 2.

4   Mix the nuts, candied fruit, dried figs, mixed peel, spices and
flour together well in a large bowl.

5   Place the sugar, honey and butter in a heavy-bottomed
saucepan and cook over a medium heat until the mixture
reaches 116°C (240°F) on a thermometer, or drop a little of
the mixture into cold water and it should form a soft ball.

6   Immediately pour the syrup into the nut mixture and stir
quickly, using a wooden spoon, until well combined.

7 Working quickly, place the mixture into the prepared cake tin. The mixture will cool quickly and become very stiff, so work fast.

8 Place the cake tin in the preheated low oven and bake for 30-40 minutes, until the outside edge begins to firm up. The panforte will not colour or seem very firm, even after baking, but will harden as it cools.

9 Cool in the tin until firm. Remove gently from the tin and remove the baking parchment.

10 Before serving, dust with icing sugar. Serve in thin slices with coffee or wrap in cellophane and tie with ribbon for a gift to friends.

crostata di caterina

CHOCOLATE, RICOTTA AND ALMOND TART

SERVES 8

PASTRY

300G (10½OZ) ITALIAN '00' PLAIN FLOUR

2 LARGE FREE-RANGE EGGS

1 LARGE FREE-RANGE EGG YOLK

100G (3½OZ) GOLDEN CASTER SUGAR

2 TSP FINELY GRATED UNWAXED LEMON ZEST

A PINCH OF SEA SALT

125G (4½OZ) UNSALTED BUTTER

PASTRY CREAM

250ML (9FL OZ) WHOLE MILK

1 LARGE PIECE UNWAXED LEMON ZEST

2 LARGE FREE-RANGE EGG YOLKS

50G (1¾OZ) GOLDEN CASTER SUGAR

2 TBSP ITALIAN '00' PLAIN FLOUR

½ TSP VANILLA EXTRACT

RICOTTA FILLING

300G (10½OZ) RICOTTA CHEESE, FRESH
    IF POSSIBLE

45G (1½OZ) GOLDEN CASTER SUGAR

3 GENEROUS TBSP CHOPPED DARK CHOCOLATE
    (70% COCOA SOLIDS)

GARNISH

18 WHOLE BLANCHED ALMONDS

18 WALNUT HALVES

VANILLA ICING SUGAR (OPTIONAL)

1   Place all the pastry ingredients in the food processor and combine. Knead the dough lightly on a work surface, then wrap in greaseproof paper and chill for half an hour.

2   For the pastry cream, combine the milk and lemon zest in a medium pan and heat over a low heat until it is just below boiling. Blend the egg yolks and sugar in a medium bowl with a wire whisk. Add the flour and stir until it is dissolved. Slowly whisk one-third of the scalded milk into the egg yolk mixture. Add the remaining milk all at once and blend well.

3   Pour the mixture back into the pan and return it to the heat. Stir constantly until the custard has thickened. Remove from the heat and stir in the vanilla. Continue to stir for 1 minute. Remove the lemon zest, pour the custard into a bowl and cover with parchment to prevent a skin forming. Allow to cool.

4   For the ricotta filling, mix the ricotta, sugar and chocolate together well.

5   Preheat the oven to 200°C (400°F) gas mark 6. Put two-thirds of the pastry dough on a lightly floured surface, flour the rolling pin and roll out the pastry to about 35cm (14in) round and 5mm (¼in) thick. Carefully roll the dough on to the rolling pin, then lower into a 28cm (11in) tart tin. Gently press the dough into the corners and against the sides of the tin.

6   Trim off the excess dough, and roll a portion of the trimmings into a rope 1cm (½in) thick and 28cm (11in) long.

Place the rope across the centre of the tart to divide the shell in half.

7   Spread the pastry cream over one half of the tart shell and the ricotta filling over the other half. Use the remaining dough to make more 1cm (½in) thick ropes. Arrange over the filling in a lattice pattern. Place an almond in each square over the ricotta filling and walnut halves over the pastry cream. Bake in the centre of the oven for 40-45 minutes, or until the crust is golden. Cool and dust with icing sugar.

THIS ICE-CREAM IS PERMANENTLY SOFT BECAUSE OF THE MASCARPONE'S HIGH FAT CONTENT. *SEMIFREDDOS* ARE FOUND MOSTLY IN THE VENETO, AND THEY ARE QUITE DIFFERENT TO THE ICE-CREAMS AND SORBETS FOUND FURTHER SOUTH. IN VENICE YOU WOULD USE '*MANDORLATO*' FOR THIS, BUT THE NOUGAT KNOWN AS *TORRONE* – PACKED FULL OF DELICIOUS NUTS AND HONEY – IS MORE WIDELY AVAILABLE.

semifreddo al torroncino

SOFT NOUGAT ICE-CREAM

SERVES 6-8

3 LARGE FREE-RANGE EGGS, SEPARATED

3 TBSP CASTER SUGAR

300G (10½OZ) MASCARPONE CHEESE

100G (3½OZ) BRITTLE NOUGAT, CHOPPED

TOASTED HAZELNUTS, CRUSHED, TO GARNISH

1   In a mixing bowl, beat the egg yolks with the sugar until pale and fluffy. Add the mascarpone and keep beating, then stir in the chopped nougat.

2   In a large bowl, whisk the egg whites until firm, and fold them into the yolk mixture.

3   Line a 1kg (2¼lb) loaf tin with a large sheet of clingfilm, pushing it to the corners and sides. Pour the mixture into the tin and freeze for several hours.

4   To serve, unmould on to a serving dish. Decorate with crushed toasted hazelnuts and slice. A red berry coulis goes well with this.

THE BEST WALNUTS ARE SAID TO COME FROM THE AOSTA
VALLEY IN THE FAR NORTH. MY SISTER, WHO LIVES IN SPAIN,
HAS TWO WALNUT TREES IN HER GARDEN, AND WE QUITE
OFTEN MAKE *NOCINO*, AN ITALIAN WALNUT LIQUEUR, FROM THE
NUTS WHEN THEY ARE STILL GREEN. WE MAKE THIS TART AS
WELL, BUT LATER IN THE YEAR. WHEN POSSIBLE, USE
FRESH NUTS FOR THEIR SWEETNESS.

torta di noci

WALNUT TART

SERVES 6

PASTRY

115G (4OZ) UNSALTED BUTTER

55G (2OZ) CASTER SUGAR

2 LARGE FREE-RANGE EGG YOLKS

225G (8OZ) ITALIAN '00' PLAIN FLOUR

FILLING

85G (3OZ) CASTER SUGAR

1 TSP FRESH LEMON JUICE

4 TBSP FRAGRANT HONEY

225G (8OZ) UNSALTED BUTTER

225G (8OZ) SHELLED WALNUTS, CHOPPED

A PINCH OF SALT

TO SERVE

ICING SUGAR

MASCARPONE CHEESE

1 To make the pastry, beat together the butter and sugar until light and soft. Add the egg yolks one at a time, then mix in the flour. With your hands, bind the mixture together. Wrap in greaseproof paper and chill in the fridge for 30 minutes.

2 Meanwhile make the filling. Put all the ingredients in a saucepan, bring to the boil and boil for 2 minutes. Remove from the heat and leave to cool.

3 Preheat the oven to 200°C (400°F) gas mark 6. On a lightly floured surface, roll out the pastry and use to line a 22cm (8½in) fluted tart tin. Do not worry if the pastry cracks; just press it into the tin and patch as necessary. Trim and re-roll the trimmings for the top.

4 Spread the cooled walnut filling into the case and cover with the pastry top. Using the prongs of a fork, seal the edges together and prick the top. Bake it in the preheated oven for 30 minutes until golden. Leave to cool in the tin.

5 Before serving, dust with sifted icing sugar. Serve with a dollop of mascarpone.

zone costiere
coasts

MAINLAND ITALY – THE HIGH-HEELED BOOT ENCIRCLED BY TWO SEAS, THE MEDITERRANEAN AND THE ADRIATIC – HAS WELL OVER 1500 MILES OF COASTLINE. MOST OF THE 18 ITALIAN REGIONS HAVE ACCESS TO THE SEA, WHILE FOUR (PIEDMONT, LOMBARDY AND TRENTINO–ALTO ADIGE IN THE NORTH, AND UMBRIA IN THE MIDDLE OF THE 'CALF') ARE LANDLOCKED. AS A RESULT, SEAFOOD HAS BEEN A MAJOR PART OF THE ITALIAN DIET FOR CENTURIES. AS WITH ALL STRANDS OF ITALIAN COOKERY, THOUGH, THE SEAFOOD DISHES DIFFER ENORMOUSLY FROM EACH OTHER. HISTORY HAS PLAYED A PART IN THIS: THE INDIVIDUAL CITY STATES THAT FORMED ITALY BEFORE THE UNIFICATION OF THE 19TH CENTURY EACH HAD THEIR OWN CUISINES AND MANY HAD ABSORBED THE INFLUENCES OF VARIOUS INVADERS AND RULERS OVER THE CENTURIES.

GEOGRAPHY AND CLIMATE AFFECT THE TYPES OF SEAFOOD FOUND AS WELL AS THE INGREDIENTS WITH WHICH THEY ARE COOKED. FOR INSTANCE, IN THE WATERY LAGOONS AND RIVER MOUTHS OF THE NORTH, IN FRIULI AND ROMAGNA, EELS FEATURE IN THE CUISINES. THE FLAT, WATERY PLAIN OF THE VALLEY OF THE PO IS WHERE ITALY'S RICE IS GROWN, SO SEAFOOD DISHES IN THE VENETO ARE SERVED WITH A RISOTTO RATHER THAN WITH THE PASTA OF FURTHER SOUTH. IN THE NORTH, HERBAL FLAVOURINGS SUCH AS SAGE AND ROSEMARY ARE USED. IN THE SOUTH, THE BOLDER OREGANO AND MARJORAM MATCH UP TO THE BRIGHT SUNSHINE, AND ALMOST ALL SAVOURY DISHES ARE ENLIVENED BY FRESH OR DRIED CHILLI. THERE TOO, BECAUSE OF THE CLIMATE, THE BEST TOMATOES IN THE WORLD ARE GROWN, AS ARE AUBERGINES, PEPPERS AND COURGETTES, AND THESE ARE USED IN SEAFOOD DISHES MORE THAN IN THE COOLER NORTH.

ALL MARITIME COUNTRIES (EXCEPT, SURPRISINGLY, BRITAIN) HAVE A BASIC SEAFOOD SOUP-STEW, AND ITALY'S ARE PRIME EXAMPLES OF THE GENRE. THE NAMES, HOWEVER, DIFFER FROM REGION TO REGION, AS DO FLAVOURINGS. THE *BRODETTO* OF THE ADRIATIC IS BASICALLY THE SAME CONCEPT AS THE *ZUPPA DI*

COZZE OR *VONGOLE* OF NAPLES, OR THE *CACCIUCCO* OF LIVORNO IN TUSCANY. THE LIGURIAN VERSION IS KNOWN AS *BURRIDA*, WHICH REVEALS A CLOSE RELATIONSHIP WITH THE *BOURRIDE* OF PROVENCE, NOT TOO FAR TO THE WEST. BUT THE *BRODETTO* OF VENICE CONTAINS NO TOMATO, AS WOULD ONE FURTHER SOUTH, AND THAT OF ROMAGNA IS FLAVOURED WITH VINEGAR (BALSAMIC VINEGAR BEING ONE OF THE MOST FAMOUS REGIONAL INGREDIENTS). THE *BRODETTO* OF THE MARCHE IS ENRICHED WITH SAFFRON, WHILE IN EXAMPLES FURTHER SOUTH, PARTICULARLY IN ABRUZZI, CHILLI – OR *DIAVOLILLO* – IS THE PREDOMINANT FLAVOURING.

MANY ITALIAN SEAFOOD DISHES REVEAL CULINARY INFLUENCES FROM OTHER CULTURES. TUNA AND SWORDFISH DISHES OF THE SOUTH AND SICILY USE DRIED FRUIT AND PINE NUTS, FLAVOURINGS INTRODUCED BY THE ARABS. THE FAMOUS MARINATED FISH DISHES ARE ALSO ARABIC IN ORIGIN AND AGAIN DIFFER IN NAME THROUGHOUT THE COASTAL AREAS. *IN SAOR* IS THE NAME USED IN THE VENETO, WHILE IN LOMBARDY IT IS *IN CARPIONE*, AND IN THE MARCHE AND SICILY *A SCAPECE*.

PERHAPS THE MOST ASTOUNDING 'ABSORPTION', THOUGH, IS THAT OF SALTED AND DRIED COD, *BACCALÀ* AND *STOCCAFISSO* RESPECTIVELY. COD IS NOT FOUND IN THE MEDITERRANEAN BUT, SINCE AT LEAST THE 16TH CENTURY, IT HAS BEEN IMPORTED IN ITS PRESERVED FORM FROM SCANDINAVIA. THIS IS THE FISH, ALONG WITH PRESERVED ANCHOVIES AND FISH ROES, THAT TENDS TO BE EATEN IN AREAS FAR FROM THE COAST.

ITALIAN COASTLINES MEAN MUCH MORE THAN SEAFOOD, THOUGH, AS THE PORTS WERE ONCE THE CONDUITS FOR MANY INFLUENCES. VENICE USED TO BE THE WORLD'S RICHEST CITY, THANKS TO ITS ROLE IN THE SPICE AND SUGAR TRADES, AND SPICES AND SWEET THINGS ONCE FEATURED STRONGLY IN ITALIAN FOOD. WHEN THE NEW DRINK, COFFEE, WAS INTRODUCED FROM THE EAST, VENICE WAS THE FIRST TO TAKE TO IT (DESPITE CHURCH DISAPPROVAL), OPENING THE WEST'S FIRST COFFEE HOUSE IN THE EARLY 17TH CENTURY.

THE WATERS OF THE MEDITERRANEAN ARE SAID TO PRODUCE SOME OF THE WORLD'S FINEST SHELLFISH, CEPHALOPODS AND CRUSTACEANS. THESE ARE CELEBRATED BY EVERYONE, RICH AND POOR, ALL ALONG ITALY'S COASTLINES. THERE'S A SEAFOOD RESTAURANT IN VERONA, RUN BY FRIENDS OF MY FATHER, WHERE YOU MUST DON A PLASTIC BIB (COMPLETE WITH PRINTED-ON BOW-TIE AND BUTTONS) BEFORE WORKING YOUR WAY THROUGH UP TO 10 COURSES – LAUGHING, TALKING, MUNCHING, CRUNCHING, SPLASHING AND BREAKING SHELLS OPEN WITH YOUR HANDS.

FISH MARKETS IN THE SOUTH ARE OPEN AT NIGHT, READY FOR WHEN FISHERMEN RETURN WITH THEIR CATCH, AND THEY HAVE MANY EAGER CUSTOMERS. SHELLFISH AND CRUSTACEANS MUST BE FRESH, ESPECIALLY IF EATEN RAW. IN THE VENETO, TRY SCALLOPS, SCAMPI, BABY CUTTLEFISH IN THEIR OWN INK, SPIDER CRABS AND *MOLECHE* (LIKE THE AMERICAN SOFT-SHELLED CRABS, BATTERED AND DEEP-FRIED). IN NAPLES, TASTE CLAMS, IN ABRUZZI RAW BABY SQUID, IN PUGLIA OYSTERS AND OCTOPUS. EVERYWHERE YOU FIND A FISH SOUP THAT CONTAINS SEAFOOD. WHETHER AS *ANTIPASTO*, WITH PASTA OR AS A MAIN COURSE, SEAFOOD IS AN ITALIAN FAVOURITE.

frutti di mare

SEAFOOD

IN ITALY, 'MEZZOGIORNO' HAS TWO MEANINGS: 'NOON' AND 'THE SOUTHERN REGIONS OF ITALY, WHICH ARE THE SUNNIEST'. THIS SALAD CELEBRATES ALL THOSE ELEMENTS, USING CAPERS FROM THE ISLANDS AND PRAWNS FROM THE RICH SEAS ALL AROUND. YOU CAN FIND MANY PRAWNS IN THE SHOPS THESE DAYS, BUT DO TRY TO BUY THEM RAW. THEY WILL BE MUCH BETTER IF COOKED AT HOME AND THEN MIXED WITH THEIR AROMATICS WHILE STILL WARM.

insalata mezzogiorno

PRAWN, ARTICHOKE AND ROASTED TOMATO SALAD

SERVES 6

4 TBSP SALTED CAPERS

12 BABY ARTICHOKES

SEA SALT AND FRESHLY GROUND BLACK PEPPER

36 RAW PRAWNS IN THE SHELL

2 BAY LEAVES

6 TBSP EXTRA VIRGIN OLIVE OIL

1 GARLIC CLOVE, PEELED AND CRUSHED

A HANDFUL OF FRESH FLAT-LEAF PARSLEY, CHOPPED

1 LEMON, SLICED

6 OVEN-ROASTED TOMATOES

1 TSP WHITE WINE VINEGAR

1   Soak the capers in lukewarm water for 20 minutes, changing the water two or three times. Drain.

2   Remove the tough outer leaves of the artichokes and trim off the leaf tips. Cut the artichokes in half and cut out the choke with a small knife. Bring abundant salted water to the boil. Drop in the artichokes and cook for about 10 minutes, until they are tender. Drain and allow to cool.

3   Cook the prawns with the bay leaves in lots of boiling water for a few minutes. Drain, shell and place in a large bowl. While still warm, season with 2 tbsp of the olive oil, the garlic, parsley and capers.

4   Place the prawns in the centre of a platter and surround them with the artichokes, lemon slices and roasted tomatoes. Sprinkle with vinegar, the remaining olive oil, salt and pepper, and serve.

ALONG THE COASTLINES OF ITALY, ESPECIALLY IN THE SUMMER, YOU WILL FIND MANY CLASSIC LIGHT SEAFOOD RECIPES – EXACTLY WHAT YOU WANT WHEN IT'S WARM. YOUR BODY NEEDS FRESH, CLEAN, CRISP FLAVOURS, WHICH IS WHAT THIS SALAD – INSPIRED BY A DISH ENJOYED IN A FASHIONABLE RESORT IN NORTHERN ITALY – PROVIDES. SERVE WITH TOASTED BREAD RUBBED WITH GARLIC AND A GLASS OF PROSECCO. LUMP CRABMEAT IS AVAILABLE IN ITALY, SAVING YOU FROM COOKING YOUR OWN AND PICKING OUT ALL THE FLESH.

insalata di granchi

CRAB SALAD

SERVES 4

1 BUNCH ROCKET

1 HEAD RADICCHIO

500G (1LB 2OZ) COOKED CRABMEAT, PICKED
   OVER (SEE NOTE)

2 AVOCADOS, STONED, PEELED AND SLICED

2 TOMATOES, CUT INTO WEDGES

6 TBSP EXTRA VIRGIN OLIVE OIL

JUICE OF 2 LEMONS

SEA SALT AND FRESHLY GROUND BLACK PEPPER

1 Wash and dry the rocket well and divide between four plates. Core the radicchio and shred. Add to the rocket.

2 Place some rocket and radicchio on each plate, then mound a quarter of the crabmeat on top. Surround with some of the avocado and tomato.

3 In a small bowl, whisk together the olive oil, lemon juice and some salt and pepper. Drizzle over the salads and serve.

Note: When in season, freshly cooked crabmeat makes this salad even more special. Put 10-12 live blue crabs into abundant boiled salted water, bring back to the boil, then simmer for 10 minutes. Cool and remove the meat from the shell with a nutcracker or mallet.

THIS RECIPE CELEBRATES ALL THE WONDERFUL SOUTHERN ITALIAN FLAVOURS. IT IS TRUE FISHERMAN'S FOOD, UNUSUAL AND SUBSTANTIAL, WITH THE CARBOHYDRATE PASTA AND BEANS ENHANCED BY THE DELICATE CLAM FLAVOUR. IN SOUTHERN ITALY THIS CLASSIC SOUP IS OFTEN PREPARED WITH PEPERONCINO (DRIED CHILLI), WHICH GIVES IT A DELIGHTFUL PIQUANCY.

pasta e fagioli con le vongole

PASTA, BEAN AND CLAM SOUP

SERVES 6

200G (7OZ) DRIED CANNELLINI BEANS, SOAKED
  OVERNIGHT

1 BOUQUET GARNI (2 SPRIGS ROSEMARY, 3 BAY
  LEAVES, 3 SPRIGS THYME, 3 SPRIGS PARSLEY)

6 TBSP OLIVE OIL

2 GARLIC CLOVES, PEELED AND CHOPPED

1 CELERY STALK, CHOPPED

1 CARROT, PEELED AND CHOPPED

1 MEDIUM ONION, PEELED AND CHOPPED

1 SPRIG FRESH ROSEMARY, LEAVES CHOPPED

4 FRESH SAGE LEAVES, CHOPPED

1 TSP DRIED CHILLI (*PEPERONCINO*)

4 RIPE PLUM TOMATOES, CHOPPED

250ML (9FL OZ) VEGETABLE OR FISH BROTH
  (SEE PAGES 188 AND 189)

200G (7OZ) DRIED PASTA (MACARONI)

SEA SALT AND FRESHLY GROUND BLACK PEPPER

EXTRA VIRGIN OLIVE OIL TO DRIZZLE

CLAM SAUCE

24 VONGOLE OR CLAMS (VENUS ARE BEST),
  CLEANED

A LITTLE FLOUR

4 TBSP OLIVE OIL

1 GARLIC CLOVE, PEELED AND CHOPPED

A HANDFUL OF FRESH FLAT-LEAF PARSLEY,
  CHOPPED

1   Wash the clams in plenty of cold water, then keep them immersed in cold water along with a little flour. This will make them spit out any sand. Discard any with damaged shells or that refuse to close when tapped on the edge of the sink.

2   Drain the cannellini beans and put into a large pot of cold water to cover. Add the bouquet garni and bring to the boil. Boil vigorously for 10 minutes, skim off any scum, then lower the heat and simmer for 30 minutes, until the beans are soft. Drain and discard the herbs.

3   In a large saucepan, heat the olive oil. Add the garlic, celery, carrot, onion, rosemary, sage and chilli (if using), and cook until lightly golden. Add the chopped tomatoes, cover and simmer for 20 minutes on a very low heat.

4   Purée half the beans in a food processor. Add to the vegetables, along with the remaining beans, the broth and pasta, and simmer for 10 minutes.

5   Meanwhile, make the clam 'sauce'. In a large frying pan heat the olive oil, and cook the garlic and clams on a high heat until the clams open (this should take minutes only). Sprinkle with the parsley.

6   Add the clam sauce to the soup with all the liquid and check for seasoning. Ladle the soup into individual dishes, and add a dash of fine extra virgin olive oil and maybe some parsley.

THIS SIMPLE RECIPE IS PROBABLY ENJOYED TWICE A WEEK IN ITALY DURING THE
SEASON, IN THE SUMMER. IT'S ONE OF MY GRANDFATHER'S FAVOURITE TREATS.
THERE IS A LOT OF CONTROVERSY IN ALL COASTAL AREAS AS TO WHETHER THE
CLAMS SHOULD BE COOKED WITH TOMATO, 'CON POMODORO', OR SERVED 'IN
BIANCO', WITHOUT. FOR SUBTLETY, I WOULD ALWAYS CHOOSE 'IN BIANCO'. LOOK
FOR SMALL CLAMS FOR THIS DISH.

spaghetti alla vongole in bianco

SPAGHETTI WITH CLAMS IN WINE

SERVES 6

3KG (6½LB) SMALL CLAMS

400G (14OZ) SPAGHETTI

SEA SALT AND FRESHLY GROUND BLACK PEPPER

3 GARLIC CLOVES, PEELED AND CHOPPED

4 TBSP OLIVE OIL

100ML (3½FL OZ) DRY WHITE WINE

3 SMALL DRIED CHILLIES (PEPERONCINO),
    CRUMBLED

A HANDFUL OF FRESH FLAT-LEAF PARSLEY,
    CHOPPED

1   Wash the clams in plenty of cold water, as described in the
    recipe on page 79.

2   While the spaghetti cooks until *al dente* in plenty of vigorously
    boiling salted water, fry the garlic in the olive oil in a very
    large pan. Add the clams, wine and chilli, cover and cook
    until the clams open. Season with salt and pepper.

3   Drain the pasta and serve immediately with the clams on top.
    Scatter with the parsley.

GARGANELLI, A PASTA SPECIALITY OF ROMAGNA, LOOKS LIKE A QUILL WITH RIDGES ON IT. IT'S MADE FROM A SMALL SQUARE OF PASTA WHICH IS ROLLED ON SOMETHING LIKE A COMB (TO GET THE RIDGES) SO THAT IT LOOKS LIKE PENNE. YOU CAN MAKE IT AT HOME – AND YOU WON'T FIND A BETTER EARLY SUMMER SAUCE FOR IT THAN THIS ONE.

garganelli con sugo di asparagi gamberetti e pomodori

GARGANELLI WITH ASPARAGUS, PRAWNS AND TOMATOES

SERVES 4

375G (13OZ) *GARGANELLI* PASTA

SEA SALT AND FRESHLY GROUND BLACK PEPPER

SAUCE

400G (14OZ) THIN ASPARAGUS, CLEANED

55G (2OZ) UNSALTED BUTTER

250G (9OZ) RAW PRAWNS IN THE SHELL

400G (14OZ) RIPE TOMATOES, CUBED,
   SEEDS DISCARDED

1 GARLIC CLOVE, PEELED AND FINELY CHOPPED

1 TBSP EACH OF FINELY CHOPPED FRESH THYME
   AND MARJORAM

A HANDFUL OF FRESH FLAT-LEAF PARSLEY,
   FINELY CHOPPED

1   To prepare the sauce, cut off the asparagus tips 5cm (2in) from the top and set aside. Slice the stems into discs about 1cm (½in) thick.

2   Melt the butter in a large frying pan over a medium heat. Add the asparagus discs, 3 tbsp water, and some salt to taste. Reduce the liquid slightly by turning up the heat for 4 minutes. Add the prawns and tomatoes and cook for 2 more minutes. Add the garlic.

3   Cook the pasta in the usual way. When the pasta has only 2-3 minutes left to cook, add the reserved asparagus tips.

4   Drain the pasta and the asparagus tips. Toss the pasta with the prawn sauce and add the herbs. Mix well and serve.

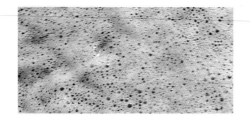

MUSSELS ABOUND ON THE EAST COAST OF ITALY, AND THE BEST ARE SAID TO COME FROM PUGLIA, A REGION RULED FOR YEARS BY THE NORMANS, ANGEVINS AND SPANISH. THIS CASSEROLE IS A REFLECTION OF ITS CHEQUERED HISTORY. '*TIELLA*', THE NAME OF THE COOKING POT AS WELL AS THE DISH, IS CLOSELY RELATED TO 'PAELLA' (AND INDEED TO THE '*TIAN*' OF SOUTHERN FRANCE, WHERE THE SPANISH ALSO HAD INFLUENCE). THERE ARE MANY SIMILAR LAYERED DISHES IN THIS PART OF THE WORLD, ONE OF WHICH USES POTATOES AND SQUID. THE DOUBLE CARBOHYDRATE OCCURS FURTHER NORTH TOO: IN LIGURIA THERE IS A DISH OF POTATO, GREEN BEANS, PESTO AND *TROFIE* PASTA.

tiella di patate, riso e cozze

POTATO, RICE AND MUSSEL CASSEROLE

SERVES 4

750G (1LB 10OZ) MUSSELS, CLEANED

3 MEDIUM ONIONS, PEELED AND THINLY SLICED

4 POTATOES, PEELED AND THINLY SLICED

150G (5½OZ) ARBORIO RICE, UNCOOKED

SEA SALT AND FRESHLY GROUND BLACK PEPPER

A LARGE HANDFUL OF FRESH FLAT-LEAF
   PARSLEY, FINELY CHOPPED

3 GARLIC CLOVES, PEELED AND SLICED

EXTRA VIRGIN OLIVE OIL

4 RIPE TOMATOES, CUT INTO STRIPS

600ML (1 PINT) WATER

1 Preheat the oven to 180°C (350°F) gas mark 4.

2 Discard any mussels with damaged shells or that refuse to close when you tap them on the edge of the sink. Put the mussels in a large pan and add a little water. Cover and bring to the boil, shaking the pan. As they open, remove from the heat. Cool a little, then extract the flesh from the shells. Discard the shells.

3 In a medium-sized baking dish layer half the onions, then half the potatoes, then half the mussels and then all the rice. Sprinkle with salt and pepper and half the parsley and garlic. Drizzle with olive oil.

4 Repeat the layering process with the remaining ingredients until the baking dish is full. Lay the tomato strips on top and add the water.

5 Bake in the preheated oven for 45 minutes. While baking, add more water if the casserole gets too dry inside.

THE SCALLOPS FROM THE ADRIATIC ARE THE TASTIEST IN THE WORLD, AND THE
VENETIANS KNOW HOW TO MAKE THE BEST USE OF THEM. THEY ARE BROUGHT IN
FRESH OFF THE BOATS EVERY DAY AND THE FINEST OF THEM ARE DIVER-CAUGHT.
EITHER LINGUINE OR TAGLIATELLE CAN BE USED FOR THIS DISH, AS BOTH GO WELL
WITH THE RICHNESS AND MEATY FLAVOUR OF THE SAUCE.

WE USE BREADCRUMBS A LOT IN ITALY TO ADD TEXTURE. THERE'S OFTEN STALE
BREAD IN THE ITALIAN KITCHEN, SOME OF IT SIMPLY GROUND AFTER BEING DRIED
IN THE OVEN, SOME TOSSED IN OIL BEFORE USE, AS HERE.

tagliatelle e cappe sante alla veneziana

TAGLIATELLE AND SCALLOPS VENETIAN STYLE

SERVES 4

12 SCALLOPS, OUT OF THEIR SHELLS,
    CORALS DISCARDED
350G (12OZ) TAGLIATELLE
SEA SALT AND FRESHLY GROUND BLACK PEPPER
125ML (4FL OZ) OLIVE OIL
55G (2OZ) DRIED WHITE BREADCRUMBS
A HANDFUL OF FRESH FLAT-LEAF PARSLEY,
    CHOPPED
2 GARLIC CLOVES, PEELED AND CRUSHED

1   Rinse the scallops quickly under cold water, then pat dry with
    kitchen paper. Cut into small pieces.

2   Put a large pan of salted water on the heat and cook the pasta
    in the usual way until *al dente*.

3   Meanwhile, put half of the olive oil in a small frying pan.
    When the oil is hot, add the breadcrumbs and stir-fry until
    golden. Set them aside.

4   Heat the remaining olive oil in a large frying pan. Add the
    parsley, garlic and scallops and stir-fry for 30 seconds, until
    the scallops start to turn opaque.

5   Drain the pasta and turn it immediately into the frying pan.
    Lift the linguine high so that every strand is coated in oil.
    Top with the fried breadcrumbs and serve at once.

ALL AROUND THE COASTLINES OF ITALY THERE ARE VERSIONS OF THIS CASSEROLE. THIS ONE COMES FROM AMALFI, NEAR WHERE I WAS BORN. IT IS A CELEBRATION OF THE BEST OF THE SEA IN ALL ITS GLORY. SERVE IT WITH LOTS OF GOOD COUNTRY BREAD TO MOP UP THE DELICIOUS JUICES.

conchiglie gratinate

BAKED MIXED SEAFOOD

SERVES 6

OLIVE OIL

12 MUSSELS, CLEANED

24 CLAMS, CLEANED

7 SLICES SLIGHTLY DRY, FIRM-TEXTURED
  WHITE BREAD

4 MEDIUM GARLIC CLOVES, PEELED AND FINELY
  CHOPPED

6 LARGE RAW PRAWNS, PEELED AND DE-VEINED

SEA SALT AND FRESHLY GROUND BLACK PEPPER

3 MEDIUM PLUM TOMATOES, CORED, SEEDED
  AND CUT INTO 1CM (½IN) DICE

A HANDFUL OF FRESH FLAT-LEAF PARSLEY,
  CHOPPED

450G (1LB) ASSORTED WHITE-FLESHED FISH,
  SKINNED, BONED AND CUT INTO CHUNKS OF
  5 X 1CM (2 X ½IN)

1   Preheat the oven to 200°C (400°F) gas mark 6. Oil six individual baking dishes or a single gratin dish that is large enough to hold the fish and seafood in a single layer.

2   Discard any mussels or clams that have broken shells or that do not close when you tap them against the side of the sink. Put the mussels and clams in a large pan and add a little water. Bring to the boil, shaking the pan and, as soon as they open, remove from the heat. Cool a little and remove the flesh from the shells. Discard the shells but keep the liquid. Strain the liquid through a fine sieve.

3   Discard the crusts from the bread and cut the bread into 1cm (½in) dice for the croûtons. Heat 3 tbsp of the olive oil in a large non-stick pan over a medium heat. Add half the garlic and stir. Add half the bread and brown lightly on all sides, tossing frequently. Transfer to a large bowl. Heat 3 more tbsp of olive oil, add the remaining garlic and bread, and brown in the same way.

4   Butterfly the prawns, arrange them outer-side-down on a work surface, and flatten them slightly with a mallet. Season with salt and pepper. Spoon 1 tsp of diced tomato on to the centre of each prawn and sprinkle with some of the parsley, reserving some of both. Roll up the prawns towards the tail to enclose the filling and hold closed with a wooden toothpick.

5   Use half of the croûtons to arrange a border around the edge
    of the chosen dish(es). Place the fish, prawns and molluscs in
    a single layer within the border, dividing the mixture evenly.

6   Season with salt and pepper. Add the remaining tomatoes and
    parsley to the croûtons left in the bowl. Pour the clam and
    mussel juices over the croûtons and toss. Scatter this mixture
    over the fish and shellfish. Bake for 20 minutes in the
    preheated oven or just until cooked through.

ITALIANS LOVE FISH: THEY TALK ABOUT IT CONSTANTLY, EAT IT CONSTANTLY, AND PROBABLY EVEN DREAM ABOUT IT. IN FACT, ITALIANS PERCEIVE THE VALUE OF FOOD FROM LAND AND SEA IN EQUAL MEASURE, AND THERE'S RELATIVELY LITTLE DIFFERENCE BETWEEN THE BASIC INGREDIENTS DEEMED FIT FOR THE RICH AND POOR. THIS IS NOW, OF COURSE; AT ONE TIME BOTH MEAT AND FISH COULD ONLY BE ENJOYED BY THE RICH – BY THE ARISTOCRACY AND THE CARDINALS....

THE KEY FISH OF THE ITALIAN SEAS ARE TUNA AND SWORDFISH CAUGHT AROUND SARDINIA AND SICILY, SOLE FROM THE ADRIATIC, SEA BASS AND MACKEREL FROM ALL OVER, AND SARDINES AND ANCHOVIES (AND, EVEN SMALLER, WHITEBAIT FROM CALABRIA). FISH ARE COOKED SIMPLY, OFTEN WITH JUST A DASH OF LEMON AND OIL, OR WITH A FEW ADDED – USUALLY ARAB-INFLUENCED – FLAVOURINGS. MANY FISH ARE USED IN THE FAMOUS FISH SOUPS, THE OLDEST AND BEST OF WHICH IS CLAIMED BY LIVORNO (LEGHORN) IN TUSCANY: THEIR *CACCIUCCO* IS A THICK FISH STEW WITH CHILLI AND AS MANY DIFFERENT FISH VARIETIES AS THERE ARE 'C' LETTERS IN THE NAME.

pesce

FISH

TUNA CAN BE FOUND ALL ALONG THE COASTLINES OF ITALY, BUT IT IS MOST COMMON IN THE WARM WATERS OF THE SOUTH. I CAN GET IT EASILY IN TUSCANY, MOSTLY COMING FROM ELBA. THIS NAPLES RECIPE HAS A GOOD DINNER-PARTY FEEL, AND THE ANCHOVIES DO GREAT FAVOURS TO THE TUNA, GIVING IT A TANGY FRESHNESS. IN LIVORNO (LEGHORN) A LITTLE FURTHER UP THE COAST, PEAS ARE ADDED TO THIS TOMATO SAUCE.

tonno fresco al pomodori

FRESH TUNA WITH TOMATOES

SERVES 4

1 X 600G (1LB 5OZ) PIECE FRESH TUNA

SEA SALT AND FRESHLY GROUND BLACK PEPPER

PLAIN FLOUR, FOR DUSTING

2 TBSP OLIVE OIL

55G (2OZ) BLACK OLIVES, PITTED

A HANDFUL OF FRESH FLAT-LEAF PARSLEY,
    CHOPPED

SAUCE

1 TBSP OLIVE OIL

1 SMALL ONION, PEELED AND CHOPPED

2 GARLIC CLOVES, PEELED AND CHOPPED

3 ANCHOVY FILLETS, MASHED

5 TBSP WHITE WINE

500G (1LB 2OZ) RIPE TOMATOES, SKINNED AND
    ROUGHLY CHOPPED

1 BAY LEAF

1 For the sauce, heat the olive oil in a saucepan, fry the onion well and then add the garlic, mashed anchovy fillets and wine. Bubble briskly until the wine has almost evaporated.

2 Add the tomato to the pan with the bay leaf and some pepper to taste. Simmer until reduced to a sauce consistency.

3 Meanwhile, season the piece of tuna fish and dust with flour.

4 Heat the olive oil in a casserole and fry the fish slowly until golden on both sides. Pour the tomato sauce over, cover with the lid, and simmer gently for 20-30 minutes. Add the olives and parsley, then serve.

THE PEOPLE OF LIGURIA EAT VERY LITTLE FISH. HOWEVER, THIS RECIPE IS ONE OF THE FEW THAT HAVE BECOME ASSOCIATED WITH THE REGION. THE SAUCE IS SIMPLE, AND THE MEATINESS OF THE ANCHOVIES AND DRIED MUSHROOMS COMPLEMENTS THE FISH WELL. IT'S A QUICK RECIPE, IDEAL FOR TODAY'S BUSY LIFESTYLES – AND IT'S HEALTHY AND DELICIOUS TOO!

tonno in padella

TUNA WITH DRIED CEP AND ANCHOVY SAUCE

SERVES 4

4 FRESH TUNA STEAKS, ABOUT 600G (1LB 5OZ)
    IN TOTAL
3 TBSP OLIVE OIL
JUICE OF 1 LEMON

SAUCE

25G (1OZ) DRIED CEPS (PORCINI)
2 GARLIC CLOVES, PEELED AND CRUSHED
A HANDFUL OF FRESH FLAT-LEAF PARSLEY,
    CHOPPED
A FEW SPRIGS OF FRESH MARJORAM
6 ANCHOVIES, DRAINED
1 TBSP SALTED CAPERS, RINSED
3 TBSP OLIVE OIL
1 TBSP PLAIN FLOUR
150ML (5FL OZ) DRY WHITE WINE
SEA SALT AND FRESHLY GROUND BLACK PEPPER

1   Soak the dried ceps in cold water for 15 minutes. Drain and dry on paper towels.

2   Put the ceps on a board with the garlic, parsley, marjoram, anchovies and capers and chop the whole lot together. The garlic absorbs the oils of the herbs, becoming less pungent in the process.

3   Heat the olive oil in a large sauté or frying pan and add the porcini mixture. Sauté for 2 minutes, stirring frequently. Blend in the flour, cook for about 1 minute, and add the wine. Boil for 3-4 minutes then add some salt and pepper. If the sauce seems thick, add 4-5 tbsp boiling water.

4   Remove the skin from the tuna steaks if it is still on. Rinse and dry the steaks with kitchen paper. Heat the olive oil in a frying pan, and cook the steaks for 2-3 minutes on each side, depending on thickness.

5   Spoon the sauce over the steaks, drizzle with lemon juice and serve immediately.

MINT FEATURES A LOT IN THE COOKING OF SOUTHERN ITALY, AN IDEA BROUGHT IN
BY THE NORTH AFRICANS. IT IS USED IN CONJUNCTION WITH FISH, COURGETTES
AND TOMATOES. MINT'S FRESH FLAVOUR BLENDS BEAUTIFULLY WITH THE SUBTLE
FISH HERE. THE RECIPE COMES FROM AMALFI, WHERE THE COOKING IS VERY
SIMPLE. YOU COULD COOK THE FISH ON A BARBECUE.

pesce alla griglia con salsa di menta

GRILLED FISH WITH MINT SAUCE

SERVES 4-6

1 WHOLE SEA BASS, ABOUT 1.2–1.4KG (2¾-3¼LB),
    SCALED AND GUTTED

SEA SALT

1 MEDIUM GARLIC CLOVE, PEELED AND
    CHOPPED

A HANDFUL EACH OF FRESH FLAT-LEAF PARSLEY
    AND MINT, CHOPPED

3-5 TSP OLIVE OIL, PLUS EXTRA FOR OILING

2-3 TSP ITALIAN '00' PLAIN FLOUR

GOOD EXTRA VIRGIN OLIVE OIL FOR ANOINTING
    AT THE END

MINT SAUCE

175ML (6FL OZ) EXTRA VIRGIN OLIVE OIL

1 SMALL GARLIC CLOVE, PEELED AND FINELY
    CHOPPED

25ML (1FL OZ) WHITE WINE VINEGAR

40ML (1½FL OZ) LEMON JUICE

A LARGE HANDFUL OF FRESH MINT LEAVES,
    CHOPPED

1   Make the mint sauce at least one hour before serving.
    Combine the olive oil, garlic, vinegar, lemon juice and some
    salt to taste in a medium bowl. Blend well with a whisk and
    stir in the mint.

2   Preheat the grill so that it's at the correct temperature at least
    15 minutes before serving. Oil the grill-pan to prevent sticking.

3   Rinse the fish in cold water and dry it with kitchen paper.
    Season the cavity with salt. Combine the garlic, parsley and
    mint. Push the mixture into the cavity and drizzle the cavity
    with 1 tsp of the olive oil. Season the top surface of the fish
    with salt, dust with 1 tsp of the flour through a small sieve,
    and drizzle with some more of the olive oil.

4   Place the fish under the grill for 8-10 minutes, or until the
    top is cooked through. To test for doneness, insert a small
    paring knife into the fleshiest part of the fish; it should be
    flaky and opaque. Turn the fish, using a large metal spatula,
    sprinkle the top with salt, flour and oil and grill the other
    side for 8-10 minutes or until thoroughly cooked.

5   Transfer to a large serving platter, drizzle with extra virgin
    olive oil, and serve with the mint sauce.

SOLE TENDS TO BE QUITE SMALL IN ITALY, BUT IT IS DELICIOUS. IT SHOULD BE COOKED SIMPLY, AS IT IS IN THIS RECIPE. IN THE SOUTH IT IS FELT THAT FISH AND OLIVES HAVE A NATURAL AFFINITY, AND I THINK THEY GO SUPERBLY TOGETHER, WITH THE OLIVES ADDING TEXTURE TO THE FISH.

sogliole alla pugliese

OVEN-BAKED SOLE WITH OLIVES

SERVES 4

4 DOVER SOLE OF ABOUT 200G (7OZ) EACH,
    GUTTED

2 TBSP OLIVE OIL

125ML (4FL OZ) WATER

1 LEMON

1 GARLIC CLOVE, PEELED AND CHOPPED

A HANDFUL OF FRESH FLAT-LEAF PARSLEY,
    FINELY CHOPPED

SEA SALT AND FRESHLY GROUND BLACK PEPPER

30 BLACK OLIVES

1   Preheat the oven to 200°C (400°F) gas mark 6.

2   Clean the soles. Place in a large baking tray with the olive oil, water, the juice of half the lemon, the garlic and parsley. Lightly season with salt and pepper and cover with foil.

3   Bake in the preheated oven for 12 minutes. Remove the dish from the oven and leave to rest for 2 minutes.

4   Arrange the soles in a serving dish with the olives, and garnish with the remaining half lemon, sliced.

THE VENETIAN *SAOR* IS ESSENTIALLY THE SAME AS THE '*IN CARPIONE*' OF
NEAPOLITAN AND LOMBARDAN COOKING AND THE '*IN SCAPECE*' OF SICILY AND THE
MARCHES. IN THIS CASE, HOWEVER, GOLDEN RAISINS, PINE NUTS AND CINNAMON
ARE ADDED, REVEALING THE ARABIC INFLUENCE. THE FISH IS MARINATED IN
VINEGAR FOR A DAY BEFORE IT IS EATEN.

sarde in saor

SOUSED SARDINES

SERVES 6 AS AN ANTIPASTO

1KG (2¼LB) FRESH SARDINES, GUTTED

125G (4½OZ) ITALIAN '00' PLAIN FLOUR

OLIVE OIL FOR DEEP-FRYING

SEA SALT AND FRESHLY GROUND BLACK PEPPER

50ML (2FL OZ) EXTRA VIRGIN OLIVE OIL

2 ONIONS, PEELED AND THINLY SLICED

250ML (9FL OZ) RED WINE VINEGAR

A PINCH OF GROUND CINNAMON

2 TBSP PINE NUTS

2 TBSP RAISINS, SOAKED FOR 10 MINUTES IN
   LUKEWARM WATER THEN DRAINED

1   Clean the sardines and remove the heads. Open the fish flat,
    wash and dry them, then dredge with flour.

2   Deep-fry the fish in very hot olive oil until crisp (about 3
    minutes), then cool.

3   Put the fish in a suitable non-reactive container and combine
    with the rest of the ingredients. Leave for a day for the
    flavours to infuse and sweeten the fish, then enjoy.

LIGURIA IS NOT KNOWN FOR FISH DISHES, DESPITE ITS LONG CURVING COASTLINE, BUT THIS IS THE BEST-KNOWN OF ITS FISH RECIPESO. I MADE THIS FOR THE PHOTO SHOOT, AND THE WHOLE TEAM SAT OUTSIDE EATING IT ON A BAKING HOT DAY. IT'S MORE OF A LATE SPRING DISH THAN A SUMMER DISH, BUT WE ENJOYED IT NONE THE LESS.

lacerti con piselli

MACKEREL WITH PEAS

SERVES 4

900G (2LB) FRESH PEAS IN THE POD

4 TBSP OLIVE OIL

5 TBSP CHOPPED FRESH MINT

A HANDFUL OF FRESH FLAT-LEAF PARSLEY,
   ROUGHLY CHOPPED

1 TBSP CHOPPED FRESH MARJORAM

1 GARLIC CLOVE, PEELED AND FINELY CHOPPED

SEA SALT AND FRESHLY GROUND BLACK PEPPER

4 MACKEREL, ABOUT 200G (7OZ) EACH, GUTTED
   AND HEADS REMOVED

4 TBSP TOMATO PASSATA

1   Pod the peas. Choose a large sauté pan, which can later contain the fish, and add the olive oil, 4 tbsp of the mint, half the parsley and all the marjoram and garlic. Let them sauté for about 1 minute, then add the peas and 4-5 tbsp hot water. Season well with salt and pepper, cover the pan and cook gently for 5 minutes.

2   Meanwhile, wash and dry the fish and sprinkle some salt and pepper inside them.

3   Stir the passata into the peas and lay the fish on top. Cover the pan tightly with foil and cook on top of the stove for about 10-12 minutes, or until by lifting a side of the fish with a flat knife you can see that the flesh is white and opaque next to the bone, from which it comes easily away. Then, and only then, is the fish ready. You might have to add a little more hot water during the cooking – just keep an eye on the pan; minimum liquid means maximum flavour.

4   Transfer the fish to a serving platter and surround them with the pea mixture. Scatter the remaining parsley and mint all over and serve.

FOR ITALIANS, DRINKING COFFEE IS LIKE A RELIGIOUS CEREMONY. THE 'BARISTA' (BARMAN) IN CHARGE OF ANY ONE OF THE GREAT COFFEE MACHINES THAT TAKE PRIDE OF PLACE IN EVERY BAR TENDS HIS MACHINE WITH CARE, POLISHING ITS GLEAMING FLANKS, NURTURING IT, PERSUADING IT TO PRODUCE – UNDER NOISILY HISSING PRESSURE – THE DARK, AROMATIC, SLIGHTLY BITTER ESPRESSO THAT IS THE FAVOURED DRINK AT BREAKFAST, MID-MORNING AND AFTER BOTH LUNCH AND DINNER. MAINLY BECAUSE THE BEANS ARE ROASTED FOR LONGER, COFFEE IN ITALY ALWAYS TASTES BETTER TO ME THAN COFFEE ELSEWHERE.

COFFEE WAS INTRODUCED TO ITALY BY THE ARABS IN THE 16TH CENTURY. THEY WERE ALSO INSTRUMENTAL IN BRINGING IN MANY OF THE SPICES THAT ONCE FEATURED CONSIDERABLY IN ITALIAN COOKERY. TRADE IN CINNAMON, NUTMEG, CLOVES AND SAFFRON MADE VENICE THE RICHEST CITY ON EARTH AT ONE TIME, AND THE SPICES STILL FLAVOUR MANY DISHES, ALTHOUGH IN MORE MODERATION NOW. IT IS CHILLI, THOUGH – A MUCH LATER IMPORT FROM THE NEW WORLD – THAT IS THE PRIME SPICE IN ITALIAN COOKING, PARTICULARLY IN THE SOUTH.

caffé e spezie

COFFEE AND SPICES

'FRITTO MISTO', OR 'MIXED FRIED FOOD', IS FOUND ALL OVER ITALY. IT CONSISTS OF SMALL MORSELS OF VEGETABLES IN BATTER OR BREADCRUMBS, WHICH ARE DEEP-FRIED AND EATEN STRAIGHT AWAY. IN EMILIA-ROMAGNA AND PIEDMONT, THEY OFTEN USE SMALL PIECES OF MEAT, POULTRY OR OFFAL; IN PUGLIA AND ELSEWHERE ALONG THE COASTS, THEY USE SMALL FISH SUCH AS ANCHOVIES, SQUID AND SARDINES. BUT IN MOST PLACES, AND PARTICULARLY IN CAMPANIA, YOU WILL FIND FRITTO MISTO OF VEGETABLES, AS HERE, SOMETHING I COOK AND EAT WITH MY STUDENTS IN TUSCANY FOR LUNCH. (IN THE VERY SHORT SEASON, YOU COULD ALSO INCLUDE COURGETTE FLOWERS.) THE CHILLI AND CLOVES ADD AN EXTRA PUNGENCY TO THE ACCOMPANYING TOMATO SAUCE.

fritto misto con salsa di pomodoro

FRIED VEGETABLES WITH TOMATO SAUCE

SERVES 6

OLIVE OIL FOR DEEP-FRYING

PLAIN FLOUR FOR DUSTING

1KG (2¼LB) MIXED VEGETABLES (E.G. PEPPERS,
    AUBERGINES, ASPARAGUS, COURGETTES),
    CUT INTO STRIPS OF ABOUT 5CM (2IN)

SAUCE

2 TBSP OLIVE OIL

2 SHALLOTS, PEELED AND FINELY CHOPPED

2 GARLIC CLOVES, PEELED AND FINELY CHOPPED

500G (1LB 2OZ) RIPE TOMATOES, CHOPPED

3 TSP DRIED CHILLI (*PEPERONCINO*)

4 CLOVES

SEA SALT AND FRESHLY GROUND BLACK PEPPER

A HANDFUL OF FRESH FLAT-LEAF PARSLEY,
    FINELY CHOPPED

BATTER

300ML (10FL OZ) MILK

1 MEDIUM EGG YOLK

½ TSP SEA SALT

125G (4½OZ) SELF-RAISING FLOUR

1 To make the sauce, heat the olive oil in a pan and cook the shallot and garlic for 3-4 minutes until they begin to soften. Add the tomatoes, chilli, cloves, salt and pepper. Simmer gently for 20 minutes, or until thick and pulpy. Set aside, picking out the cloves if you can.

2 For the batter, whisk together the milk, egg yolk and salt in a large bowl. Sift the flour into the bowl and whisk together to make a batter.

3 Heat 4cm (1½in) of olive oil in a deep pan. Spread a little flour on a plate. Dip the vegetable pieces one at a time into the flour then into the batter to coat. Carefully drop into the oil in batches and cook for about 2 minutes, until golden. Drain well on kitchen paper.

4 Stir the fresh parsley into the sauce and serve with the warm *fritto misto*.

THIS IS A NEAPOLITAN ICE-CREAM MADE WITH CREAM, CUSTARD AND GROUND COFFEE. A *SPUMONE* IS A LIGHTER, SOFTER ICE-CREAM THAT WILL NEVER ENTIRELY FREEZE BECAUSE OF ITS FAT CONTENT. THE USE OF GROUND COFFEE MAY SOUND UNUSUAL, BUT I GUARANTEE YOU'LL BE DELIGHTED BY THE RESULTS. YOU COULD SERVE THIS WITH THE ALMOND BISCUITS ON PAGE 60.

spumone di caffè

COFFEE AND CINNAMON ICE-CREAM

SERVES 6

4 LARGE FREE-RANGE EGG YOLKS

115G (4OZ) CASTER SUGAR

½ TSP FRESHLY GROUND CINNAMON

3 TBSP FINELY GROUND ITALIAN COFFEE

750ML (1 PINT 7FL OZ) DOUBLE CREAM

1   Put the egg yolks, sugar, cinnamon and coffee in a heatproof bowl and beat well together.

2   Place the bowl over a saucepan of simmering water and, using an electric whisk, mix until doubled in volume. Remove the bowl from the heat and continue whisking until cool.

3   Whip the cream until it just holds its shape, then fold into the egg mixture.

4   Pour the mixture into an ice-cream machine and freeze according to the manufacturer's instructions. Alternatively pour the mixture into a shallow freezer container and freeze, covered, for an hour. Turn the mixture into a chilled bowl and whisk until smooth. Return to the container, freeze again until mushy, then whisk again. Return to the freezer to become firm. Cover the container with a lid.

THESE LIGHT AND DELECTABLE BISCUITS ARE AN INVENTION OF MY
GRANDMOTHER. SHE ALWAYS LIKED TO PRESENT THEM TO US AFTER OUR SIESTA,
AND THEY WERE A GREAT KICK-START TO THE REST OF THE DAY. AS SHE WAS SUCH
A ROMANTIC, SHE CALLED THEM 'COFFEE KISSES'. THEY ARE SIMPLE TO MAKE,
WITH A WONDERFUL TEXTURE, AND FILLED WITH A CREAMY COFFEE CUSTARD.

baci di caffè

COFFEE KISSES

MAKES 6 BISCUITS

2 LARGE FREE-RANGE EGGS

125G (4OZ) CASTER SUGAR

125G (4OZ) SELF-RAISING FLOUR

4 TBSP CORNFLOUR

ICING SUGAR FOR DUSTING

FILLING

3 LARGE FREE-RANGE EGG YOLKS

55G (2OZ) CASTER SUGAR

2 TBSP PLAIN FLOUR OR ITALIAN '00' PLAIN
   FLOUR

225ML (8FL OZ) MILK

1 TBSP FINELY GROUND ITALIAN COFFEE

125ML (4FL OZ) DOUBLE CREAM

1 Preheat the oven to 180°C (350°F) gas mark 4. Grease several
   baking trays.

2 Put the eggs and sugar into a mixing bowl and beat together
   until thick and creamy. Sift the flour and cornflour together,
   then fold through the egg mixture.

3 Spoon heaped tbsps of the mixture on to the baking trays,
   allowing plenty of space for spreading. You should have
   12 kisses.

4 Bake in the preheated oven for 10 minutes, until the kisses are
   pale golden and firm to the touch. Transfer to a wire rack and
   leave to cool.

5 To make the filling, whisk together the egg yolks, sugar and
   flour until thick and creamy. Gently heat the milk and coffee
   together in a saucepan, but do not allow to boil. Gradually
   whisk the milk mixture into the egg mixture. Return the
   mixture to the saucepan and heat, stirring, until it thickens.
   Remove from the heat, cover with parchment paper and leave
   to cool.

6 Whisk the cream until stiff. When the filling mixture is cold,
   fold in the cream.

7 To serve, spread the filling over the flat side of half of the
   coffee kisses and top each with another coffee kiss. Dust with
   icing sugar and serve immediately.

WHEN I'M TEACHING IN ITALY I AM CONSTANTLY BEING ASKED FOR RECIPES FOR
COFFEE DESSERTS AND CAKES. THE ITALIANS LOVE COFFEE, DRINK IT A LOT, AND
USE IT IN SWEET COOKING. THIS IS AN INVENTION OF MINE, BUT IT IS VERY
TRADITIONALLY ITALIAN IN FEEL. IT'S RICH, SWEET AND STICKY, PERFECT FOR MY
STUDENTS WHO ARE ALWAYS WANDERING AROUND LOOKING FOR A *MERENDA*, OR
SNACK, AT ABOUT FOUR IN THE AFTERNOON...

torta di caffè

COFFEE CAKE

SERVES 12-16

5 LARGE FREE-RANGE EGG WHITES

250G (9OZ) CASTER SUGAR

200G (7OZ) GROUND ALMONDS

55G (2OZ) TOASTED FLAKED ALMONDS TO
  DECORATE

ICING

190G (6½OZ) UNSALTED BUTTER

375G (13OZ) ICING SUGAR

75ML (2½FL OZ) STRONG ESPRESSO COFFEE

A SPLASH OF COFFEE LIQUEUR (TIA MARIA)

1 Preheat the oven to 180°C (350°F) gas mark 4. Line a 25cm
   (10in) springform cake tin with baking parchment.

2 Whisk the egg whites until stiff, then gradually add the caster
   sugar, beating well between each addition to form a stiff,
   glossy meringue mixture. Gently fold in the ground almonds.

3 Spoon into the lined cake tin and bake in the preheated oven
   for 30 minutes. Allow to cool completely before icing.

4 Meanwhile, to make the coffee butter cream icing, soften the
   unsalted butter and beat thoroughly. Then add the icing sugar,
   a little at a time, being careful not to beat the mixture too fast
   and risk losing the sugar over the side of the bowl. Once all
   the sugar is thoroughly incorporated, gradually drizzle in the
   cold espresso and then the liqueur and combine.

5 Smooth the icing over the top and side of the meringue cake
   and decorate with the flaked almonds.

THIS IS A CLASSIC ITALIAN CAKE, AND I HAVE THE MOST WONDERFUL MEMORIES OF IT BEING SERVED AT SPECIAL FAMILY GATHERINGS AND FEAST DAYS. MY SISTER'S BIRTHDAY IS IN AUGUST, SO THAT WAS ONE ANNUAL EXCUSE (OF MANY) FOR INDULGING OURSELVES. IT CAN ALSO BE USED FOR AN ITALIAN WEDDING CAKE.

torta della mia nonna

MY GRANDMOTHER'S TART

SERVES ABOUT 16

CAKE

6 LARGE FREE-RANGE EGGS

175G (6OZ) CASTER SUGAR

175G (6OZ) ITALIAN '00' PLAIN FLOUR

CONFECTIONER'S CUSTARD

2 TBSP ITALIAN '00' PLAIN FLOUR OR
　　CORNFLOUR

2 TBSP CASTER SUGAR

1 LARGE FREE-RANGE EGG, BEATEN

FINELY GRATED ZEST OF 1 UNWAXED LEMON

½ TSP VANILLA EXTRACT

300ML (10FL OZ) MILK

BUTTER CREAM

175G (6OZ) UNSALTED BUTTER

175G (6OZ) ICING SUGAR

1 MEDIUM FREE-RANGE EGG

1 TBSP CASTER SUGAR

100ML (3½FL OZ) COLD ESPRESSO COFFEE

1　Preheat the oven to 190°C (375°F) gas mark 5. Grease and line a 30cm (12in) cake tin and dust with extra flour.

2　To make the cake, put the eggs and sugar in a bowl and stand over a saucepan of gently simmering water. Using an electric whisk, whisk until thick and creamy. Gently sift in the flour a little at a time and fold it in. Pour into the prepared tin. Bake for 18-20 minutes, until risen and golden. Turn out and cool on a wire rack.

3　To make the custard, in a small bowl mix together the flour or cornflour, sugar, egg, lemon zest and vanilla extract. Gently heat the milk in a saucepan but do not allow to boil. Gradually pour into the egg and flour mixture. Return to the saucepan and heat very gently, stirring constantly with a wooden spoon until the mixture thickens. Remove from the heat and place a piece of parchment paper over the custard to prevent a skin forming. Leave to cool.

4　To make the butter cream, in a bowl beat together the butter and icing sugar. In a separate bowl, beat the egg with the caster sugar. Add the egg and sugar mixture to the butter mixture. Using an electric whisk, gently add the coffee and mix until thick and creamy.

5　To assemble the cake, cut the cake horizontally into three. Spoon the custard on one layer and spread the butter cream on the second layer. Sandwich the cake slices together.

TOPPING

3 TBSP RUM

300ML (10FL OZ) DOUBLE CREAM

A FEW DROPS OF VANILLA EXTRACT

5 TBSP TOASTED FLAKED ALMONDS OR
   HAZELNUTS

SEASONAL FRUIT SUCH AS PEACHES,
   NECTARINES, STRAWBERRIES AND
   RASPBERRIES

6 Gently pour over the rum to soak into the cake.

7 Whip the cream with the vanilla extract until the cream
just holds its shape, then use to cover the top and sides of
the cake. Carefully press the nuts on to the sides and
decorate the top with the prepared fresh fruit. Chill
before serving.

pianure

plains

ALTHOUGH ITALY IS LARGELY MOUNTAINOUS, WHERE THERE IS A MOUNTAIN THERE IS ALSO USUALLY A PLAIN. OFTEN THE MOUNTAINS LITERALLY DROP STRAIGHT INTO THE SEA, BUT IN SOME PLACES THERE IS A GENTLE INCLINE, CREATING MANY COASTAL PLAINS WHERE FRUIT ORCHARDS, VEGETABLES, GRAPE VINES AND OLIVES ARE CULTIVATED.

THE PRINCIPAL FLAT LANDS OF ITALY ARE IN THE NORTH, IN THE GREAT ALLUVIAL PLAIN THAT IS FOUND ON EITHER SIDE OF THE RIVER PO, FLOWING FROM THE ALPS IN THE WEST TO THE ADRIATIC. HERE THE MAJORITY OF THE COUNTRY'S GRAINS ARE GROWN: WHEAT FOR BREAD AND PASTA, MAIZE FOR POLENTA, AND BARLEY, BUCKWHEAT AND FARRO (A FORM OF SPELT OR WHEAT). THE AREA WAS ONCE MARSHY, BUT MUCH OF THE LAND WAS DRAINED AROUND THE 12TH CENTURY IN ORDER TO CREATE VAST TRACTS OF LAND ON WHICH GRAINS COULD BE GROWN.

GRAINS HAVE BEEN THE FOOD OF ITALY'S RURAL POOR FOR CENTURIES. BEFORE THE ARRIVAL OF MAIZE, BROUGHT TO THE COUNTRY IN THE 16TH CENTURY FROM THE NEW WORLD BY COLUMBUS, A BASIC GRAIN PORRIDGE OR 'PULS' WOULD HAVE BEEN MADE FROM MILLET, BUCKWHEAT, WHEAT OR OTHER GRAINS. MAIZE WAS ACCEPTED READILY, AND THE PORRIDGE MADE WITH IT, POLENTA, IS STILL A MUCH-LOVED STAPLE, PARTICULARLY IN THE MOUNTAINOUS NORTH (THE PASTA-EATING SOUTHERNERS HAVE A DISPARAGING NAME FOR THE NORTHERN POLENTA-EATERS, *POLENTONE*). THE WHOLE NORTH OF ITALY IS PART OF WHAT HAS BEEN CALLED THE 'POLENTA, RISOTTO AND BEAN SOUP' BELT.

ITALIANS EAT GRAINS IN LARGE QUANTITIES – IN THEIR PASTAS (OF WHICH THERE ARE OVER 600 SHAPES AND REGIONAL TYPES), RISOTTOS, POLENTA AND BREADS. MANY ITALIAN SOUPS CONTAIN GRAINS, AND NO SOUP (OR INDEED MEAL) COULD BE EATEN WITHOUT BEING ACCOMPANIED BY BREAD. NOWHERE IS BREAD

MORE VALUED THAN IN ITALY, AND THERE ARE HUNDREDS OF TYPES OF REGIONAL BREADS. PIZZA WAS DEVELOPED IN NAPLES IN THE SOUTH (ALSO THE CENTRE OF MACARONI-EATING). INTERESTINGLY, NAPLES WAS ONE OF THE MAJOR POINTS OF ENTRANCE FOR UNFAMILIAR VEGETABLES IMPORTED FROM THE NEW WORLD, AND TOMATOES AND GREEN PEPPERS WERE ADOPTED AND ALLIED WITH THE PIZZA BREAD BASE.

HOWEVER, THE GREAT ITALIAN PLAINS ARE HOME TO MUCH MORE THAN GRAIN CULTIVATION. IN THE COASTAL PLAINS OF THE SOUTH, IN LAZIO, PUGLIA AND CAMPANIA, THE WATER BUFFALO – INTRODUCED TO ITALY IN THE 16TH CENTURY – EATS, WALLOWS AND PRODUCES A RICH BUT LOW-FAT MILK THAT IS USED TO MAKE THAT UNIQUE ITALIAN CHEESE, MOZZARELLA.

FRUIT AND VEGETABLES ARE GROWN ALL OVER ITALY: ON THE PLAINS, IN THE FOOTHILLS, AND OFTEN EVEN HIGHER. I'VE NOT DEVOTED A SEPARATE SECTION TO VEGETABLES AS THEY'RE FOUND IN ALMOST EVERY ITALIAN DISH. THE MORE TEMPERATE VARIETIES OF FRUIT FLOURISH IN THE NORTH, WHILE THE MORE TROPICAL AND EXOTIC APPEAR IN THE SOUTH. ON THE HIGHLY FERTILE PUGLIAN PLAINS, GRAPES, OLIVES, PEACHES, APRICOTS AND TOMATOES ARE GROWN. IN CAMPANIA, WHERE I COME FROM, MY FAMILY GROWS FRUIT FOR LOCAL AND INTERNATIONAL CONSUMPTION. I GREW UP KNOWING ALL SORTS OF THINGS ABOUT GROWING PEARS, PLUMS, APRICOTS, ORANGES AND LEMONS. I KNEW – AND NOT JUST IN THEORY – HOW TO GRAFT LEMONS TO GET A THINNER SKIN, MORE JUICE, OR A FRUIT SO SWEET THAT YOU COULD EAT IT LIKE AN ORANGE. THE SMELL OF LEMONS, OF THE OILS IN THE SKIN OR OF THE BLOSSOM, INSTANTLY REMINDS ME OF HEAT AND HAPPINESS, AND VIRTUALLY REPRESENTS THE ESSENCE OF ITALY. MY GRANDFATHER USED TO SAY THAT THE LEMON IS A TRUE MEDICINE; AND I AGREE WITH HIM AND USE IT ON A DAILY BASIS. IT'S A VITAL FLAVOURING IN MY COOKING AND IN ITALIAN COOKING IN GENERAL.

ITALIANS EAT A LOT OF GRAINS, MOST OF WHICH ARE GROWN IN THE VALLEY OF THE RIVER PO IN THE NORTH. WHEAT COMES IN TWO FORMS: SOFT WHEAT MAKES THE BREADS; HARD OR DURUM WHEAT (ALSO KNOWN AS SEMOLINA) MAKES THE DRIED AND FRESH PASTA. SOME PASTA IS A SIMPLE AMALGAM OF FLOUR AND WATER, SOME IS EGG-ENRICHED, AND SOME IS COLOURED. WHEAT IS ALSO USED IN CAKES, PIZZA DOUGHS AND GNOCCHI. 'GNOCCHI' MEANS 'LITTLE LUMPS' (OR DUMPLINGS), WHICH IS EXACTLY WHAT THEY USUALLY ARE. WHEN POTATOES WERE INTRODUCED TO ITALY IN THE 16TH CENTURY, POTATO GNOCCHI BECAME POPULAR, BUT GNOCCHI CAN ALSO BE MADE FROM RICOTTA, SEMOLINA OR SPINACH.

ANOTHER FOOD INTRODUCED TO ITALY IN THE 16TH CENTURY, MAIZE, WAS USED INSTEAD OF OTHER GRAINS AS THE BASE OF THE PORRIDGE WE NOW KNOW AS POLENTA. IT IS EATEN 'WET' OR 'SET' AND GRILLED OR FRIED, MOSTLY EATEN IN THE NORTH.

FARRO OR SPELT (OF THE SAME GENUS AS COMMON WHEAT) WAS ONCE EUROPE'S STAPLE GRAIN, BUT WITH THE DEVELOPMENT OF MODERN FARMING IT BECAME UNPOPULAR. TODAY IT IS BEING CULTIVATED AND ENJOYED AGAIN.

pasta, gnocchi, polenta e farro

PASTA, GNOCCHI, POLENTA AND FARRO

THE REGION OF CAMPANIA HAS BEEN BLESSED WITH ALL OF THE ELEMENTS FOR GROWING FRUIT AND VEGETABLES OF FINE QUALITY – RICH VOLCANIC SOIL, A PROFUSION OF BRIGHT SUNSHINE AND A GENTLE CLIMATE – AND THE REGION'S DIET RELIES HEAVILY ON THEM. CAMPANIA'S SAN MARZANO TOMATO, A THICK-FLESHED COOKING TOMATO, IS VALUED AROUND THE WORLD AND HAS BECOME THE SYMBOL OF THE REGION.

penne con pomodoro al gratin

PENNE WITH ROASTED TOMATOES

SERVES 4

125G (4½OZ) SALTED CAPERS, RINSED

2 MEDIUM GARLIC CLOVES, PEELED AND SLICED

A HANDFUL OF FRESH BASIL LEAVES

16 MEDIUM PLUM TOMATOES, CORED, HALVED
    LENGTHWAYS AND SEEDED

125ML (4FL OZ) OLIVE OIL

30G (1¼OZ) DRY BREADCRUMBS

SEA SALT AND FRESHLY GROUND BLACK PEPPER

900G (2LB) PENNE

TO SERVE

GRATED PARMESAN CHEESE

1   Preheat the oven to 180°C (350°F) gas mark 4 and oil two 33 x 23cm (13 x 9in) baking sheets.

2   Drain the capers and dry with kitchen paper.

3   Combine the capers, garlic and basil leaves on a cutting board and finely chop them together.

4   Arrange the tomatoes, cut side up, on the baking sheets. Sprinkle the chopped mixture over the tomatoes, drizzle with olive oil and sprinkle with the breadcrumbs. Season to taste. Roast in the preheated oven for 1 hour, or until the tomatoes are very soft, but still hold their shape.

5   Shortly before the tomatoes are ready, fill a large pot with water and bring to the boil. Add salt to taste and stir in the penne. Cook until *al dente*. Drain and transfer to a large serving bowl, spoon the tomatoes on top and toss well.

6   Serve immediately with lashings of Parmesan cheese.

lasagne tricolore

SPINACH, FENNEL AND TOMATO LASAGNE

SERVES 8

8 RIPE PLUM TOMATOES

SEA SALT AND FRESHLY GROUND BLACK PEPPER

2 GARLIC CLOVES, PEELED AND FINELY CHOPPED

1 TBSP OLIVE OIL

2 FENNEL BULBS

500G (1LB 2OZ) SPINACH, WASHED, TOUGH
    STALKS REMOVED

FINELY GRATED ZEST OF 1 UNWAXED LEMON

125G (4½OZ) PARMESAN CHEESE, FRESHLY
    GRATED

350G (12OZ) RICOTTA CHEESE

BUTTER FOR GREASING

9 SHEETS PRE-COOKED LASAGNE

175G (6OZ) MOZZARELLA CHEESE, SLICED

A HANDFUL OF FRESH BASIL

BECHAMEL SAUCE

600ML (1 PINT) MILK

1 ONION, PEELED AND QUARTERED

1 BAY LEAF

6 BLACK PEPPERCORNS

45G (1½OZ) BUTTER

35G (1¼OZ) ITALIAN '00' PLAIN FLOUR

FRESHLY GRATED NUTMEG

1   Begin by infusing the milk for the béchamel sauce. Put the milk with the onion, bay and peppercorns in a pan, bring just to the boil, turn off the heat, cover and leave to infuse while you prepare the other ingredients.

2   Preheat the oven to 180°C (350°F) gas mark 4. Cut the tomatoes in half and arrange them, cut side up, on a baking tray. Sprinkle them with salt and pepper, garlic and olive oil and bake them until softened and wilted (about 35 minutes).

3   Pull off the tough outer layers of the fennel bulbs and cut the fennel tops where they meet the bulbs. Slice about 4mm (⅛in) from the root end, and cut lengthways into thin slices. Drop the fennel into plenty of salted simmering water and cook for about 5 minutes, until the root ends of the slices feel tender but firm when prodded with a fork. Drain well.

4   Put the spinach in a pan with 1cm (½in) of water. Cover the pan and cook the spinach over a high heat until the leaves start to wilt. Stir, replace the cover, and cook until completely wilted (which will take only a minute or two). Drain in a colander and, when cooled slightly, squeeze dry in your hands. Form the spinach into small marble-sized balls.

5   Beat the lemon zest and about half of the Parmesan cheese into the ricotta and correct the seasoning.

6   Now finish the béchamel sauce. Melt the butter, stir in the flour and cook gently for about 1 minute, stirring all the time,

until the mixture is quite smooth and pale yellow. Take the pan off the heat and pour in the milk through a sieve to strain out the flavourings. Whisk briskly until smooth. Put the pan back on the heat and bring back to the boil, whisking all the time, until the sauce thickens. Season with salt, pepper and nutmeg, and simmer gently for a minute or two.

7   To assemble the lasagne, butter a baking dish about 23 x 23cm (9 x 9in). Pour half the sauce into the bottom of the dish and cover with a single layer of pasta. Spread the pasta with half of the ricotta mixture and arrange the tomato halves, sliced mozzarella, basil and fennel slices in that order evenly on top. Follow this with another layer of pasta spread with the rest of the ricotta and dot with the spinach balls. Arrange a final layer of pasta on top, pour over the rest of the sauce and sprinkle evenly with the remaining grated Parmesan.

8   Put the lasagne into the oven and cook until golden and bubbling (about 30 minutes). Serve at once.

GNOCCHI ARE MADE FROM A VARIETY OF INGREDIENTS, SUCH AS POTATOES, SEMOLINA OR PUMPKIN, AND THIS IS MY TAKE ON THE RICOTTA VERSION. I HAVE A PASSION FOR GREEN FOOD, AND THESE LITTLE DUMPLINGS ARE LIGHT, TASTY, PUNGENT WITH THE SAGE, SIMPLE, AND REASSURINGLY GREEN! I COOK THIS WHEN I GO TO VISIT MY SISTER AND HER FIVE NAUGHTY (BUT NICE) CHILDREN.

gnocchi di spinaci, piselli e ricotta

SPINACH, GREEN PEA AND RICOTTA GNOCCHI

SERVES 4

225G (8OZ) FRESH SPINACH LEAVES

225G (8OZ) FRESH SHELLED PEAS

1 TBSP TORN FRESH SAGE LEAVES

2 LARGE FREE-RANGE EGGS

200G (7OZ) RICOTTA CHEESE

A PINCH OF FRESHLY GRATED NUTMEG

SEA SALT AND FRESHLY GROUND BLACK PEPPER

85G (3OZ) PARMESAN CHEESE, FRESHLY GRATED

3 TBSP FRESH BREADCRUMBS

5 TBSP PLAIN FLOUR

TO SERVE

25G (1OZ) UNSALTED BUTTER

8 FRESH SAGE LEAVES

1 Wash the spinach leaves and remove the tough stems. Put into a large saucepan with only the water still clinging to the leaves after washing. Cover and cook for about 5 minutes, stirring once or twice. Drain, cool a little and then squeeze out all the water using your hands. The spinach must be completely dry.

2 Cook the peas in a little water until just tender (about 8 minutes). Drain well. Put the spinach, peas and sage in a food processor and chop finely.

3 Lightly beat the eggs and add to the spinach mixture with the ricotta, nutmeg, salt, pepper, half the Parmesan cheese, breadcrumbs and nearly all the flour. Mix well, adding more flour if necessary. The mixture should be firm enough for a spoon to stand up in.

4 Using well-floured hands, take a piece of the mixture about the size of a heaped dessertspoon, and roll lightly into a small oval. Repeat until all the mixture is used up.

5 Bring a large saucepan of water to the boil, then reduce the heat. Drop in the gnocchi, a few at a time, and cook for 4-5 minutes or until they rise to the surface. Remove from the pan with a slotted spoon and drain. Put in a warmed serving dish, cover and keep warm.

6 Melt the butter with the sage leaves and pour over the gnocchi. Serve sprinkled with the remaining Parmesan.

THE MAIZE FOR POLENTA MAY BE GROWN ON THE PLAINS OF ITALY, BUT POLENTA IS ALSO POPULAR IN THE MOUNTAINS BECAUSE IT CAN SUSTAIN YOU DURING HARD WINTERS. POLENTA HAS HAD A BAD PRESS BECAUSE BY ITSELF IT CAN BE BLAND, BUT IT HAS A MAGICAL ABILITY TO ABSORB FLAVOURS. IT CAN BE EATEN 'WET' OR SET, AS HERE, AND EVEN AS AN ALTERNATIVE TO BREAD.

spiedini di polenta

POLENTA AND ROASTED VEGETABLE SKEWERS

SERVES 6 AS AN ANTIPASTO

225G (8OZ) CHERRY TOMATOES

2 TBSP OLIVE OIL

450G (1LB) FLAT MUSHROOMS

2 SPRIGS FRESH ROSEMARY

115G (4OZ) DOLCELATTE CHEESE

FRESHLY GRATED PARMESAN CHEESE FOR
    SPRINKLING

POLENTA

750ML (1 PINT 7FL OZ) VEGETABLE BROTH
    (SEE PAGE 188) OR WATER

SEA SALT AND FRESHLY GROUND BLACK PEPPER

200G (7OZ) COARSE POLENTA

55G (2OZ) BUTTER

85G (3OZ) PARMESAN CHEESE, FRESHLY GRATED

1 GARLIC CLOVE, PEELED AND CRUSHED

1 To make the polenta, bring the broth or water and 1 tsp salt to the boil in a large saucepan. Gradually add the polenta, stirring constantly. Simmer for 30-40 minutes until the mixture comes away from the sides of the pan, stirring frequently. Add the butter, Parmesan, garlic and some black pepper.

2 Spread the hot mixture on to a dampened baking sheet to a 5mm (¼ in) thickness. Leave for about 1 hour until set.

3 Meanwhile, preheat the oven to 200°C (400°F) gas mark 6.

4 Cut the tomatoes in half and place on a baking sheet. Drizzle with a little of the olive oil. Thickly slice the mushrooms and place on a baking sheet. Sprinkle with the remaining olive oil and place some rosemary on top. Bake the tomatoes and mushrooms in the oven for 20 minutes.

5 Using a 2.5cm (1in) round cutter, cut the cold polenta into rounds. Cut the dolcelatte into cubes.

6 Thread the halved tomatoes, mushrooms, polenta rounds and cheese on to cocktail sticks or kebab sticks. Sprinkle with Parmesan cheese.

7 To serve, grill for about 7 minutes, until golden.

THE ANCIENT ROMANS USED FARRO FLOUR TO MAKE *PULS*, A SORT OF POLENTA, WHICH BECAME A BASIC STAPLE IN THEIR DIET. ALTHOUGH WHEAT DISPLACED FARRO AS THE GRAIN OF CHOICE DURING THE RENAISSANCE, TODAY IT IS ONCE AGAIN IN FASHION AND IS GROWN IN UMBRIA, LAZIO AND TUSCANY. YOU CAN USE DRIED BEANS IF YOU CAN'T GET HOLD OF FRESH, BUT BE SURE TO BOIL THEM VIGOROUSLY FOR 10 MINUTES BEFORE SIMMERING THEM.

gran farro

SPELT SOUP

SERVES 6

250G (9OZ) FRESH BORLOTTI BEANS, PODDED

250G (9OZ) FRESH CANNELLINI BEANS

250G (9OZ) FARRO

6 TBSP OLIVE OIL

1 SMALL ONION, PEELED AND FINELY CHOPPED

2 GARLIC CLOVES, PEELED AND FINELY CHOPPED

1 CELERY STALK, CHOPPED

6 FRESH SAGE LEAVES, CHOPPED

10 FRESH MARJORAM LEAVES, CHOPPED

3 RIPE PLUM TOMATOES, CHOPPED

A PINCH OF FRESHLY GRATED NUTMEG

SEA SALT AND FRESHLY GROUND BLACK PEPPER

EXTRA VIRGIN OLIVE OIL TO DRIZZLE

1 Stir the beans into a large pot filled with cold water to cover. Bring to the boil, lower the flame and simmer until the beans are tender (about 40 minutes). Drain, reserving the cooking liquid. Pass the beans through a food mill or mouli in order to obtain a purée.

2 Wash the farro in cold water, drain and pat dry.

3 In a casserole, heat the olive oil, then add the onion, garlic, celery, sage and marjoram, and sauté until lightly golden. Add the tomatoes and nutmeg and cook for 10 minutes.

4 Add the puréed beans, farro and reserved bean liquid to the vegetable mixture in the casserole. Simmer for 30 minutes, season well with salt and pepper, then simmer for an additional 10 minutes.

5 Ladle the soup into individual dishes and serve with a dash of extra virgin olive oil.

THIS IS A SPECIAL DINNER-PARTY POLENTA DISH, WHICH CAN BE MADE A DAY AHEAD, LEAVING YOU MORE TIME TO CONCENTRATE ON OTHER COURSES ON THE DAY ITSELF. NEVER ECONOMISE WHEN YOU ARE BUYING POLENTA. GET THE REAL THING, THE KIND THAT NEEDS LONG COOKING. THE INSTANT POLENTA AVAILABLE NOW IS VERY DISAPPOINTING.

polenta pasticciata

BAKED STUFFED POLENTA

SERVES 4

SEA SALT AND FRESHLY GROUND BLACK PEPPER

225G (8OZ) COARSE POLENTA

90G (3¼OZ) BUTTER

A HANDFUL OF FRESH OREGANO SPRIGS, CHOPPED

1 SMALL AUBERGINE

1 RED PEPPER

1 COURGETTE

450G (1LB) FLAT FIELD MUSHROOMS

3 TBSP OLIVE OIL, PLUS EXTRA FOR DRIZZLING

25G (1OZ) ITALIAN '00' PLAIN FLOUR

300ML (10FL OZ) MILK

55G (2OZ) BLUE CHEESE, E.G. GORGONZOLA

A HANDFUL OF FRESH FLAT-LEAF PARSLEY, FINELY CHOPPED

115G (4OZ) PARMESAN CHEESE, FRESHLY GRATED

1 Dampen a 1kg (2¼lb) loaf tin. In a large heavy saucepan bring 1.5 litres (2¾ pints) water to simmering point. Add 1½ tsp salt to the water, then pour in the polenta, letting it run through your fingers in a thin stream, stirring all the time to prevent lumps forming. Cover and simmer for 40 minutes, stirring vigorously every 5 minutes. The polenta is cooked when it comes away from the sides of the saucepan.

2 Now add 55g (2oz) of the butter and stir in well. Add some salt and pepper and the chopped oregano. Stir until the butter has melted. Pour into the loaf tin and leave to set for 20-30 minutes.

3 Preheat the oven to 200°C (400°F) gas mark 6.

4 Slice the aubergine lengthways, sprinkle with salt, place in a colander, cover and weigh down for 20 minutes.

5 Meanwhile put the red pepper in a baking tray and roast in the preheated oven for 20 minutes, until deflated, turning once during cooking. Leave to cool.

6 Trim the ends of the courgette, then slice them lengthways and slice the mushrooms. Heat the olive oil in a frying pan and fry the courgette, then drain and reserve. Now fry the mushrooms until tender, season with salt and pepper and reserve. Rinse the aubergine slices, pat dry and fry until golden. Drain and reserve. When the pepper is cool, peel off the skin and chop the flesh, discarding the core and seeds.

7 Now make the sauce. In a saucepan, melt the remaining butter. Add the flour and cook the roux for 3 minutes, stirring. Remove the pan from the heat and gradually beat in the milk. Return to the heat and slowly bring to the boil, beating all the time until thickened. Stir in the Gorgonzola, mushrooms and some salt and pepper.

8 Turn the set polenta out of the tin on to a board and cut into five slices lengthways. Put one slice back in the tin, and layer the polenta with all the fillings, sauce and the Parmesan. Drizzle on some olive oil and bake in the oven at the same temperature as above for 20 minutes.

IMPASTONE MEANS TO KNEAD, AND *IMPASTOIATA* IS A MIXTURE SIMILAR TO A DOUGH. THIS DOUBLE CARBOHYDRATE DISH, SO TYPICAL OF THE NORTH OF ITALY, IS MADE TO CELEBRATE THE ARRIVAL OF THE NEW BEANS IN THE AUTUMN. IT'S A HUMBLE DISH, BUT THE FLAVOURS ARE STUNNING. THIS RECIPE USES FRESH CANNELLINI BEANS, BUT YOU CAN USE DRIED (TO COOK, SEE PAGE 79).

impastoiata
POLENTA AND CANNELLINI BEANS

SERVES 6

2 TBSP OLIVE OIL

1 SMALL ONION, PEELED AND FINELY CHOPPED

1 GARLIC CLOVE, PEELED AND FINELY CHOPPED

4 FRESH SAGE LEAVES, CHOPPED

2 SPRIGS FRESH ROSEMARY, CHOPPED

SEA SALT AND FRESHLY GROUND BLACK PEPPER

400G (14OZ) TIN CHOPPED ITALIAN TOMATOES

1.5 LITRES (2¾ PINTS) VEGETABLE BROTH (SEE PAGE 188)

225G (8OZ) COARSE POLENTA

300G (10½OZ) FRESH CANNELLINI BEANS, COOKED (SEE PAGE 119)

FRESHLY GRATED PARMESAN CHEESE

EXTRA VIRGIN OLIVE OIL

1 First make the sauce. Put the oil, onion, garlic, sage, rosemary, 1 tsp salt and plenty of pepper in a saucepan and cook for 10 minutes over a low heat. Add the tomatoes and cook until the sauce has thickened (about 20-25 minutes).

2 While the sauce is cooking, make the polenta. Heat the vegetable broth. When it begins to bubble at the side, add the polenta in a thin stream while beating hard with a wooden spoon. Cook, stirring, for 40 minutes. When the polenta has cooked and is coming away from the sides of the pan, mix in the beans and season.

3 Serve the sauce with the polenta, sprinkling Parmesan and extra virgin olive oil on top.

THE BEST MOZZARELLA, IN MY OPINION, COMES FROM MY HOME REGION OF CAMPANIA. IT IS MADE FROM THE MILK OF WATER BUFFALO THAT ROAM FREELY IN MANY AREAS OF THE SOUTH, PRINCIPALLY CAMPANIA, LAZIO AND PUGLIA (I ALWAYS FIND IT EXTRAORDINARY THAT SUCH AN INNOCENT-LOOKING CHEESE SHOULD BE THE PRODUCT OF SUCH FIERCE-LOOKING ANIMALS). THE MILK IS RICH BUT LOW IN FAT, WHICH MAKES FOR A WONDERFUL CHEESE; A MILLION TIMES MORE INTERESTING THAN THE SLAB-LIKE, PALE IMITATIONS MADE IN COUNTRIES TO THE NORTH OF EUROPE.

THE BEST WAY TO EAT A GOOD MOZZARELLA (WHICH SHOULD COME BATHING IN ITS PACKET OR TUB OF BRINE) IS WITH ONLY A FEW FLAVOURINGS. IT IS QUITE BLAND, SO DOES NEED A LITTLE HELP. GOOD RIPE TOMATOES, FRESH BASIL, SALT AND PEPPER, WITH LOTS OF EXTRA VIRGIN OLIVE OIL, MAKE FOR A WONDERFUL SALAD. BUT MOZZARELLA'S MELTING STRINGINESS ALSO MAKES IT THE IDEAL PIZZA TOPPING. IT IS ALSO FRIED, SANDWICHED BETWEEN SLICES OF BREAD, TO MAKE *MOZZARELLA IN CARROZZA* ('IN A CARRIAGE'). MY PASTRY RECIPE ON PAGE 124 IS AN EXPLORATION OF THE SAME BASIC IDEA.

mozzarella

MOZZARELLA

MOZZARELLA IS WONDERFUL ON A PIZZA, MELTING TO A LUSCIOUS STRINGINESS AND ABSORBING ALL THE ADDITIONAL FLAVOURS. HERE I'VE USED AUBERGINES WITH LOTS OF MOZZARELLA AND A MINT PESTO (YOU DON'T ALWAYS HAVE TO USE BASIL). I COOK IT OFTEN FOR MY STUDENTS IN TUSCANY, PICKING MINT FROM THE GARDEN AND PINE NUTS FROM THE SURROUNDING TREES.

pizza di melanzane e pesto di menta

MINT PESTO AND AUBERGINE PIZZA

SERVES 4

1 QUANTITY PIZZA DOUGH (SEE PAGE 176)

½ SMALL AUBERGINE

SEA SALT AND FRESHLY GROUND BLACK PEPPER

1 TBSP OLIVE OIL

250G (9OZ) MOZZARELLA CHEESE

MINT PESTO

A HANDFUL OF FRESH MINT, CHOPPED,
    PLUS SPRIGS TO GARNISH

55G (2OZ) PINE NUTS

55G (2OZ) PARMESAN CHEESE, FRESHLY GRATED

1 SMALL GARLIC CLOVE, PEELED

2 TBSP OLIVE OIL

1   To make the mint pesto, put the mint, pine nuts, Parmesan, garlic and olive oil in a mortar and, using the pestle, grind until the mixture is a paste.

2   Slice the aubergine into thin rings. Put the slices in a colander, sprinkle with salt, cover and weigh down. Leave for about 30 minutes.

3   Rinse the aubergine slices and pat dry with absorbent kitchen paper. Heat the olive oil in a frying pan and fry the aubergine slices until lightly golden on both sides.

4   Preheat the oven to 200°C (400°F) gas mark 6. On a very lightly floured surface, roll out the pizza dough very thinly into a round of approximately 14cm (5½in). Place on an oiled baking sheet.

5   Slice the mozzarella cheese. Spread a generous layer of mint pesto on to the pizza base, then arrange the mozzarella and aubergine slices on top. Season and add the remaining mint pesto. Bake in the oven for 20 minutes, until golden and bubbling. Serve garnished with sprigs of mint.

I CREATED THIS DISH ONE SUNDAY MORNING, WHEN I INVITED SOME FRIENDS FOR LUNCH ON THE SPUR OF THE MOMENT, AND THEN REALISED I ONLY A LITTLE CHEESE AND SOME PASTRY IN THE FRIDGE. I PICKED THE THYME AND POTATOES FROM MY GARDEN AND SET TO WORK. MY FRIENDS SEEMED TO ENJOY THIS ENORMOUSLY, DESCRIBING IT AS A 'CRUNCHY PIZZA'. IT IS BASED ON A CLASSIC DISH FROM THE ITALIAN PLAINS, WHERE YOU'LL FIND THE COUNTRY'S BEST POTATOES AND GARLIC.

mozzarella in pasta frolla

BUFFALO MOZZARELLA BAKED ON PASTRY

SERVES 6

PASTA FROLLA

125G (4½OZ) UNSALTED BUTTER

200G (7OZ) ITALIAN '00' PLAIN FLOUR

4 TBSP ICED WATER

A PINCH OF SALT

TOPPING

6 X 125G (4½OZ) BALLS BUFFALO MOZZARELLA

6 NEW POTATOES (ITALIAN SPUNTA), SCRUBBED

6 SPRIGS FRESH THYME

2 GARLIC CLOVES, PEELED AND FINELY SLICED

115G (4OZ) PARMESAN, FRESHLY GRATED

SEA SALT AND FRESHLY GROUND BLACK PEPPER

1   Place all the *pasta frolla* ingredients in a food processor and pulse until a dough forms. Wrap the pastry in foil and chill in the fridge for 45 minutes.

2   On a flat surface, roll out the dough into a rectangle measuring 20 x 40cm (8 x 16in). Chill for 30 minutes. Preheat the oven to 180°C (350°F) gas mark 4.

3   Cut the dough into six equal squares. Bake on baking sheets in the preheated oven for 15 minutes, until golden brown. Set aside and cool. Turn the oven up to 230°C (450°C) gas mark 8.

4   Cut each mozzarella ball into four slices and place on top of each square of pastry. Slice the potatoes into wafer-thin slices or blanch and then slice thinly. Layer these on top of the mozzarella with the thyme, garlic, parmesan, sea salt and a generous amount of black pepper.

5   Bake in the preheated oven for 8 minutes, until golden and bubbling.

THIS DISH IS TYPICAL OF THE SOUTH OF ITALY, AND WE OFTEN MAKE IT WITH
COURGETTES INSTEAD OF AUBERGINES. ANY FILLING CAN BE USED – YOU COULD
ADD SOME ANCHOVY, FOR INSTANCE – AND IT IS PERFECT SERVED AS A *CONTORNO*,
OR VEGETABLE COURSE.

melanzane arrotolate con mozzarella

AUBERGINE AND MOZZARELLA ROLLS

SERVES 4

2 MEDIUM AUBERGINES

SEA SALT AND FRESHLY GROUND BLACK PEPPER

OLIVE OIL FOR FRYING

300G (10½OZ) MOZZARELLA CHEESE, THINLY
   SLICED

150G (5½OZ) PARMESAN CHEESE, FRESHLY
   GRATED

A HANDFUL OF FRESH BASIL LEAVES

5 TBSP TOMATO SAUCE (SEE PAGE 188)

1 Cut the aubergines lengthways into slices about 5mm (¼in)
thick. Sprinkle with salt and weight down for 20 minutes.
Rinse the slices and pat dry.

2 Heat 2 tbsp of the olive oil in a frying pan and fry the slices of
aubergine until golden and soft on both sides (about 7
minutes altogether). Do this in batches, adding more olive oil
as needed. Drain well on kitchen paper.

3 Preheat the oven to 190°C (375°F) gas mark 5.

4 Put a slice of mozzarella cheese, a little grated Parmesan, a
basil leaf and some salt and pepper on each slice of aubergine.
Roll each one up carefully, fix with a wooden toothpick, and
put into a roasting tin.

5 Spoon a little cooked tomato sauce on top and bake in the
preheated oven for 10 minutes until bubbling.

ITALY HAS A VARIED CLIMATE FROM NORTH TO SOUTH, AND SO IS A PRIME PRODUCER OF FRUIT. TEMPERATE FRUITS, SUCH AS APPLES AND PEARS, FLOURISH IN THE COOLER PLAINS OF THE NORTH, WHILE CITRUS FRUITS ARE RAMPANT IN THE HOT SOUTH. AS I HAVE SAID, MY FAMILY WAS, AND STILL IS, ASSOCIATED WITH FRUIT GROWING AND EXPORTING. MY GRANDFATHER, WHO STARTED THE BUSINESS, GREW LEMONS AND IN SEASON WOULD BRING THEM ACROSS TO ENGLAND TO SELL TO BARS FOR THEIR GIN AND TONICS. FROM SMALL BEGINNINGS, AS THEY SAY, THE COMPANY HAS EXPANDED, AND WE STILL GROW LEMONS: THICK-SKINNED FOR *LIMONCELLO* (A WONDERFUL LEMON LIQUEUR) AND THIN-SKINNED FOR JUICING.

FIGS ARE CULTIVATED IN THE SOUTH, AND ALSO GROW WILD. RIPE FIGS PLUCKED STRAIGHT FROM THE TREE ARE HEAVENLY, BUT THEY CAN BE DRIED TOO. MANY FRUITS ARE PRESERVED IN ITALY: APRICOTS, FIGS AND PLUMS ARE DRIED; CITRUS RIND IS CRYSTALLISED FOR USE IN CAKES AND PUDDINGS; SOME FRUITS ARE COOKED DOWN TO A PASTE (QUINCE PARTICULARLY); AND SOME FRUITS ARE PRESERVED IN A SWEET-SOUR MUSTARDY SYRUP FOR THE FAMOUS PRESERVE '*MOSTARDA DI CREMONA*'.

frutta

FRUIT

THIS IS A CLASSICALLY SEASONAL ITALIAN RECIPE, MADE IN THE LATE SUMMER
WHEN THERE IS A GLUT OF COURGETTES AND LEMONS. LEMONS ARE MEDICINAL,
BUT THEY ALSO CREATE AND ADD WONDERFUL FLAVOUR, ESPECIALLY IN THIS TANGY
PESTO. THE COURGETTES CAN BE SERVED HOT OR COLD.

zucchini al limone

LEMON PESTO WITH COURGETTES

SERVES 4

8 MEDIUM COURGETTES, GRATED

4 SPRING ONIONS, FINELY CHOPPED

LEMON PESTO

JUICE AND FINELY GRATED ZEST OF 2 UNWAXED
  LEMONS

A HANDFUL OF FRESH BASIL

4 GARLIC CLOVES, PEELED

150G (5½OZ) PINE NUTS

4 TBSP EXTRA VIRGIN OLIVE OIL

SEA SALT AND FRESHLY GROUND BLACK PEPPER

3 TBSP FRESHLY GRATED PARMESAN CHEESE

1   Steam the courgettes and onions for 4 minutes.

2   Combine all the pesto ingredients in a pestle and mortar
    or food processor.

3   Combine the pesto with the courgettes and onions.

4   Heat through gently in a saucepan and serve with bread.

I MAKE NO APOLOGIES FOR INCLUDING ANOTHER COURGETTE AND LEMON DISH, FOR BOTH FOODS ARE SO TYPICAL AND REDOLENT OF THE SOUTH OF ITALY. HERE THE PEPPERY ROCKET ADDS A DIFFERENT DIMENSION, AS DOES THE SAVOURINESS OF THE PARMESAN.

carpaccio di zucchini

COURGETTE CARPACCIO

SERVES 4

500G (1LB 2OZ) SMALL YOUNG COURGETTES

150G (5½OZ) ROCKET

4 TBSP EXTRA VIRGIN OLIVE OIL

JUICE OF 1 UNWAXED LEMON, AND THE FINELY
   GRATED ZEST OF 2

SEA SALT AND FRESHLY GROUND BLACK PEPPER

100G (3½OZ) PARMESAN CHEESE, SLICED INTO
   SLIVERS

1   Bring a medium saucepan of water to the boil. Add the courgettes and boil for 3 minutes, then plunge them into cold water and pat dry. Trim the ends of the courgettes and slice at an angle into thin ovals. Place in a bowl.

2   Pick through the rocket and discard any yellow leaves. Snap off the stalks then wash and dry the leaves thoroughly.

3   Mix together the olive oil, lemon juice and zest, and some salt and pepper, and pour over the courgettes. Mix, then leave to marinate for 5 minutes. Season with salt and pepper.

4   Arrange the rocket leaves on the serving plate, put the courgettes on top and then arrange the Parmesan slivers on top of the courgettes. Add a little black pepper to taste.

LEMONS ABOUND ON THE AMALFI COAST. I INVENTED THIS RECIPE FOR MY
GRANDPA, BECAUSE HE LOVED PROFITEROLES, AND HIS BUSINESS WAS GROWING
LEMONS. I ALSO SERVED THIS LIGHT, DRAMATIC DESSERT AT MY BOYFRIEND'S
BIRTHDAY PARTY IN ENGLAND, AND IT WAS A HUGE SUCCESS.

profiteroles al limone

LEMON PROFITEROLES

SERVES 8

250ML (9FL OZ) COLD WATER

125G (4½OZ) UNSALTED BUTTER, CUT INTO
   PIECES, PLUS EXTRA FOR GREASING

1 TSP CASTER SUGAR

A PINCH OF SEA SALT

125G (4½OZ) ITALIAN '00' PLAIN FLOUR

4 LARGE FREE-RANGE EGGS

LEMON PASTRY CREAM

375ML (13FL OZ) WHOLE MILK

½ VANILLA POD

3 LARGE FREE-RANGE EGG YOLKS

125G (4½OZ) CASTER SUGAR

45G (1½OZ) ITALIAN '00' PLAIN FLOUR

FINELY GRATED ZEST OF 2 UNWAXED LEMONS

TO FINISH

250M (9FL OZ) DOUBLE CREAM

ZEST OF 1 UNWAXED LEMON, CUT INTO
   JULIENNE STRIPS, FOR GARNISH

FRESH MINT (OPTIONAL)

1 To start the lemon pastry cream, combine the milk and the vanilla pod in a medium saucepan. Heat over a medium-low heat until scalded (just up to boiling point).

2 While the milk is heating, whisk together the egg yolks and sugar in a large bowl. Add the flour and stir until it is completely dissolved. Slowly whisk one-third of the scalded milk into the egg yolk mixture. Add the remaining milk all at once and blend thoroughly.

3 Pour the mixture back into the pan and return it to the heat. Stir constantly until the pastry cream has thickened. Turn off the heat, add the grated lemon zest and continue to stir for 1 minute. Remove the vanilla pod and pour the mixture into a bowl. Place a piece of parchment paper on top in order to stop a skin forming.

4 Preheat the oven to 220°C (425°F) gas mark 7 and adjust two racks in the centre of the oven. Butter two large baking sheets.

5 To make the profiteroles, combine the cold water, butter, sugar and a pinch of salt in a medium-heavy saucepan over a

medium-low heat. Bring the mixture to the boil and melt the butter. As soon as the water reaches a boil, remove the pan from the heat.

6   Add the flour all at once and stir with a wooden spoon. When the flour is thoroughly blended in, return the pan to the flame. Stir vigorously for 1-2 minutes, or until the mixture pulls away from the sides of the saucepan, forming a ball of dough.

7   Remove the pan from the heat and rest it on a damp towel. Beat in the eggs, one at a time. Incorporate each egg thoroughly before adding the next.

8   Scrape the profiterole mixture into a piping bag fitted with a 1cm (½in) round tip. Pipe 24 small mounds of dough 4cm (1½in) in diameter and spaced about 5cm (2in) apart on to the two baking sheets. Moisten your index finger with water and gently flatten the pointed peaks.

9   Place the baking sheets in the oven, staggered so that they are not on top of each other. Bake for 20 minutes, or until golden. Reverse the position of the baking sheets after 15 minutes so the profiteroles bake evenly. Turn off the oven and cool the profiteroles thoroughly in the oven with the door slightly ajar.

10 Beat half the double cream until it is stiff. Stir this whipped cream into the lemon pastry cream to lighten it. Spoon this mixture into a piping bag fitted with a 5mm (¼in) plain tip. Make a small slit on the side of each profiterole and fill with the lightened pastry cream. Stack the profiteroles on a large platter and spoon the remaining lightly whipped double cream over. Sprinkle with the lemon zest and serve immediately. Fresh mint may be used as a garnish as well.

I FIRST MADE THIS CAKE WHEN WE HAD FAR TOO MANY FIGS IN THE GARDEN AND
SO DRIED THEM IN THE PIZZA OVEN. YOU CAN LEAVE THIS CAKE FOR A WHILE
BEFORE EATING IT, AS IT IMPROVES IN TEXTURE, BECOMING DAMPER. IT'S IDEAL
FOR TAKING ON A PICNIC AS IT'S NOT TOO STICKY OR GOOEY. IT'S ALSO RATHER
HEALTHY, PRINCIPALLY BECAUSE OF THE ENERGY-RICH FIGS, BUT ALSO BECAUSE
THE USE OF THE OIL CUTS DOWN ON MORE DAMAGING FATS.

torta di fichi

ORANGE, ALMOND AND FIG CAKE

SERVES 8

150ML (5FL OZ) OLIVE OIL, PLUS EXTRA FOR
  GREASING

10 DRIED FIGS, FINELY CHOPPED

500G (1LB 2OZ) ITALIAN '00' PLAIN FLOUR,
  PLUS 2 TBSP

2 LARGE EGGS

175G (6OZ) GRANULATED SUGAR

1 TSP GROUND CINNAMON

1½ TSP BAKING POWDER

100G (3½OZ) GROUND ALMONDS

½ TSP SEA SALT

150ML (5FL OZ) FRESH ORANGE JUICE

FINELY GRATED ZEST OF 1 UNWAXED ORANGE

55G (2OZ) SLIVERED ALMONDS

1   Preheat the oven to 180°C (350°F) gas mark 4. Oil a 20cm
    (8in) ring mould or cake tin.

2   Toss the chopped figs with the 2 tbsp flour. Beat the eggs,
    olive oil and sugar together until you have a thick and
    creamy mixture.

3   Mix the remaining flour with the cinnamon, baking powder,
    ground almonds and salt. Add the flour mixture, alternating
    with the orange juice, to the egg mixture, stirring until
    blended. Stir in the orange zest and chopped figs.

4   Pour the batter into the prepared cake tin or mould and
    sprinkle with slivered almonds. Bake in the preheated oven
    for 35 minutes. Cool in the tin.

torta di mele con prugne

APPLE AND PLUM TART

SERVES ABOUT 8

PASTRY

280G (10OZ) ITALIAN '00' PLAIN FLOUR

55G (2OZ) CASTER SUGAR, PLUS EXTRA FOR
    SPRINKLING

1 LARGE EGG, LIGHTLY BEATEN

A PINCH OF SEA SALT

100ML (3½FL OZ) WHOLE MILK, TEPID

85G (3OZ) UNSALTED BUTTER, SOFTENED

FILLING

55G (2OZ) UNSALTED BUTTER

900G (2LB) GRANNY SMITH APPLES, PEELED,
    CORED AND CUT INTO 2CM (¾IN) SLICES

450G (1LB) PLUMS, RIPE AND JUICY, HALVED
    AND STONED

140G (5OZ) CASTER SUGAR

1 TBSP LIGHT RUM

1   To make the pastry, mound the flour on a pastry board or work surface. Make a well in the centre and add the sugar, egg, salt, milk and softened butter. Blend the ingredients in the well with a fork. Gradually incorporate the flour to make a soft ball of dough. Knead the dough gently for 1 minute. Wrap the dough in clingfilm and let it rest at room temperature for at least 30 minutes (it doesn't need chilling).

2   To make the filling, melt the butter in a large pan, add the apple slices and sauté over a medium-high heat, stirring often, until the apples are *al dente*. Do not let the apples become soft. Stir in the plums and sugar, add the rum and cook until the juices have thickened. Let the mixture cool completely.

3   Preheat the oven to 190°C (375°F) gas mark 5. When the apples are cool, lightly dust the pastry board or work surface with flour. Roll out two-thirds of the dough into a 38cm (15in) round, wrap the dough round a rolling pin, then lower into a 28cm (11in) tart tin. Press the dough into the corners and against the sides of the tin. Allow the excess dough to hang over the sides of the tin. Spoon the apple mixture into the shell.

4   Roll out the remaining piece of dough into a 25cm (10in) round. Cover the apple mixture with the round of dough and fold the overhanging excess dough from the base over the top pastry round, letting the dough drape casually. Sprinkle with sugar and bake in the centre of the preheated oven for 45 minutes or until golden brown. Cool on a cooling rack.

I'VE BEEN MAKING THIS TART FOR AGES, AND I'M ALWAYS SURPRISED BY HOW
EASY IT IS AND BY HOW CRISP THE PASTRY IS. IT COMES FROM A RESTAURANT IN
ROME, WHERE THE PROPRIETRESS IS AN ENGLISHWOMAN MARRIED TO AN ITALIAN.
I GUESS THAT'S WHERE THE MARMALADE COMES FROM! ALWAYS USE THE BEST
DARK CHOCOLATE, WHICH HAS A MAGICAL AFFINITY WITH THE SWEET PEARS.

crostata di pere a cioccolato

CHOCOLATE PEAR TART

SERVES 8-12

PASTRY

55G (2OZ) UNSALTED BUTTER

115G (4OZ) PLAIN FLOUR OR ITALIAN '00' PLAIN
    FLOUR

25G (1OZ) COCOA POWDER

55G (2OZ) CASTER SUGAR

1 LARGE FREE-RANGE EGG, BEATEN

FILLING

3 TBSP ORANGE MARMALADE

2 RIPE PEARS

115G (4OZ) DARK CHOCOLATE (70%
    COCOA SOLIDS)

55G (2OZ) UNSALTED BUTTER

2 LARGE FREE-RANGE EGGS, SEPARATED

115G (4OZ) CASTER SUGAR

1   To make the pastry, rub the butter into the flour until the
    mixture resembles breadcrumbs. Sift in the cocoa powder,
    then add the sugar and enough of the beaten egg to bind the
    mixture together. Knead lightly, wrap in greaseproof paper
    and chill in the fridge for 20 minutes.

2   On a lightly floured surface, roll out the pastry and use to line
    a 20cm (8in) fluted flan tin. Cover the bottom of the pastry
    case with the marmalade.

3   Peel the pears, cut into quarters and remove the cores.
    Arrange them in the flan case.

4   Melt the chocolate and butter together over a low heat. Set
    aside to cool.

5   Preheat the oven to 180°C (350°F) gas mark 4.

6   Beat together the egg yolks and sugar until pale and fluffy.
    Fold in the chocolate mixture. Whisk the egg whites until
    stiff, then fold into the mixture.

7   Pour the mixture over the pears and bake in the oven for
    30 minutes, until firm to the touch. Serve hot or cold.

I'M PERMANENTLY UPDATING MY CHOCOLATE RECIPES, AND IN EVERY BOOK I HAVE
WRITTEN, I'VE INCLUDED A 'CHOCOLATE COLLECTION' IN MY SEARCH FOR THE
BEST-EVER CHOCOLATE CAKE. I THINK I'VE FOUND IT IN THIS TUSCAN-INSPIRED
PRUNE CAKE. I HOPE YOU LIKE IT.

torta di prugne e cioccolato

CHOCOLATE AND PRUNE CAKE WITH ESPRESSO SYRUP

SERVES 8

200G (7OZ) EXCELLENT-QUALITY PRUNES,
    HALVED AND STONED

4 TBSP BRANDY

200G (7OZ) HIGH-QUALITY CHOCOLATE, IN
    SMALL PIECES

25G (1OZ) HIGH-QUALITY COCOA POWDER

175G (6OZ) DARK MUSCOVADO SUGAR

4 LARGE FREE-RANGE EGG WHITES

75G (2¾OZ) PLAIN FLOUR

ESPRESSO SYRUP

1 TSP FINELY GROUND ESPRESSO COFFEE

25G (1OZ) CASTER SUGAR

1 TBSP LEMON JUICE

*Note: To get really rich chocolate
cakes, use dark sugars which help the
colour, taste and texture.*

1   Place the prunes in a small bowl and spoon the brandy over the
    top. Soak the prunes for 2 hours, or until the brandy is absorbed.

2   Preheat the oven to 190°C (375°F) gas mark 5. Line the base and
    sides of a 20cm (8in) spring-form cake tin with parchment paper.

3   Place the chocolate, cocoa, 150g (5½oz) of the sugar and 150ml
    (5fl oz) boiling water in a large mixing bowl. Stir until melted
    and smooth.

4   Whisk the egg whites in a separate bowl until stiff. Gradually
    whisk in the remaining sugar. Sift the flour over the mixture and
    then fold in gently using a large metal spoon, until the flour is
    nearly incorporated.

5   Stir about a quarter of the egg white mixture into the chocolate
    mixture until incorporated. Then pour the chocolate mixture
    into the remaining egg whites and carefully fold in until the
    texture becomes loose. Pour into the prepared tin.

6   Scatter the prunes over the top, then bake for 30-35 minutes, or
    until the sponge is just firm and has risen up around the prunes.
    Leave to cool in the tin – it will sink a little as it cools.

7   While the cake is cooking, make the syrup. Place the coffee and
    sugar in a small heavy-based saucepan with the lemon juice and
    150ml (5fl oz) cold water. Heat gently until the sugar has
    dissolved. Bring to the boil and cook for 3-5 minutes, until the
    mixture thickens and becomes syrupy. Strain and serve spooned
    over the cake.

laghi e fiumi
lakes and rivers

BECAUSE ITALY IS LARGELY MOUNTAINOUS, IT HAS NO LACK OF FRESH WATER IN THE FORM OF MOUNTAIN STREAMS AND RIVERS RUSHING DOWN TO THE SEA; OF INLAND AND UPLAND LAKES; AND, PARTICULARLY IN THE NORTH, THE WATERY PLAIN THAT IS THE VAST VALLEY OF THE RIVER PO AND ITS TRIBUTARIES.

IT IS IN THIS VALLEY OF THE PO THAT FRESH WATER HAS ITS GREATEST EFFECT ON ITALY'S SCENERY, AGRICULTURE AND COOKING. HERE, IN VAST ACREAGES THAT STRETCH AS FAR AS THE EYE CAN SEE, THE GOLD AND TAN OF GRAINS SUCH AS WHEAT AND BARLEY CONTRAST WITH THE FRESH GREEN, WATERY SQUARES OF THE RICE FIELDS. THE AREA WAS ONCE VERY MARSHY AND, AFTER DRAINING IN ORDER TO CULTIVATE OTHER GRAINS, WAS STILL WET ENOUGH TO SUSTAIN RICE. PIEDMONT PRODUCES SOME 60 PER CENT OF ITALY'S RICE AND, IN EVERY REGION OF THE NORTH (THE 'RISOTTO, POLENTA AND BEAN SOUP BELT' OF ITALY), RICE IS EATEN IN SOME FORM OR ANOTHER: AS RISOTTO, IN CAKES AND IN SOUPS. RISOTTO IS VIRTUALLY THE DEFINING DISH OF VENICE, THE ULTIMATE LAGOON CITY, AND THERE IT IS SERVED WITH EVERY TYPE OF SEAFOOD AND, IN EARLY SUMMER, WITH PEAS IN THE FAMOUS *RISI E BISI*. THE VENETIAN RISOTTO IS WETTER (*ALL ONDA*, LIKE A WAVE) THAN THAT OF NEIGHBOURING REGIONS SUCH AS LOMBARDY AND FRIULI-VENEZIA GIULIA, AND IN FACT IS OFTEN IDENTIFIED ON MENUS AS *MINESTRA* SOUP.

ALTHOUGH I RARELY COOK WITH FRESHWATER FISH AND SO HAVE NOT INCLUDED ANY RECIPES IN THIS BOOK, IT IS IMPORTANT TO MENTION THAT THE RIVERS, FROM NORTH TO SOUTH, YIELD FRESHWATER TROUT, PIKE, PERCH AND CARP (THERE USED TO BE STURGEON IN THE MOUTH OF THE PO, BUT SADLY NO LONGER, BECAUSE OF POLLUTION). BABY EELS OR ELVERS ARE CAUGHT AT THE MOUTHS OF SEVERAL RIVERS AS THEY ARRIVE, SWEPT FROM THEIR BIRTHPLACE IN THE SARGASSO SEA BY THE GULF STREAM. OLDER FISH ARE CAUGHT AS THEY RETURN TO THE SEA AFTER MATURING, OR AS THEY RETURN TO THEIR HOME WATERS TO

SPAWN. A FULLY MATURE FEMALE EEL, *CAPITONE*, IS A SPECIAL CHRISTMAS TREAT IN ROME AND FURTHER SOUTH. THE VALLI DI COMACCHIO IS A WATERY, SALT-MARSH AREA JUST NORTH OF RAVENNA IN EMILIA–ROMAGNA, AND THE TOWN THERE IS ACTUALLY BUILT ON A GROUP OF 13 ISLANDS, BISECTED BY CANALS AND CONJOINED BY BRIDGES. THIS IS THE FAMED ADRIATIC CENTRE OF EEL FISHING AND COOKING. EELS ARE EVEN FOUND IN UMBRIA, WHICH IS ONE OF THE FEW REGIONS IN ITALY WITH NO COASTLINE!

LAKES ARE ANOTHER GREAT SOURCE OF FRESHWATER FISH. THERE ARE THREE LAKES IN THE MIDDLE AND SOUTH OF THE COUNTRY: TRASIMENO IN UMBRIA, BRACCIANO NEAR ROME AND BOLSENA IN LAZIO. IN THE NORTH, ON THE BORDERS OF LOMBARDY AND SWITZERLAND, LIE THE MOST FAMOUS ITALIAN LAKES: GARDA, MAGGIORE, LUGANO AND COMO. MANY FISH UNKNOWN ELSEWHERE ARE CAUGHT HERE; THOSE FROM COMO AND MAGGIORE ARE OFTEN HUNG TO DRY IN THE SUN AND THEN GRILLED FOR A LOCAL SPECIALITY, *MISSOLTIT*.

IN MY OPINION THE FINEST SOFT HERBS IN ITALY GROW NEAR THE LAKES AND RIVERS. FISH – AND INDEED JUST ABOUT EVERYTHING EATEN IN ITALY – IS ALWAYS ENHANCED BY HERBS, WHETHER THEY ARE USED IN THE COOKING, ADDED AT THE END, OR MADE INTO A SHARP ACCOMPANYING SAUCE. PARSLEY, MELDED WITH THE SHARPNESS OF CAPERS AND ANCHOVIES, MAKES A WONDERFUL *SALSA VERDE* FOR GRILLED TROUT. AND BASIL, THE QUINTESSENTIAL ITALIAN HERB, IS GROWN AND ENJOYED ALL OVER THE COUNTRY, BUT PLAYS PERHAPS ITS GREATEST ROLE IN THE LIGURIAN BASIL, OIL AND PINE NUT SAUCE, PESTO.

GRAPE VINES GROW IN THE PO VALLEY AS WELL, PRODUCING SOME OF THE MOST FAMOUS AND HIGHLY REGARDED OF ITALIAN WINES. IT IS IN THE VENETO, NEAR THE TOWNS OF VALDOBBIÁDENE AND CONEGLIANO, THAT THE PROSECCO GRAPES ARE CULTIVATED TO MAKE THE GENTLE AND *SPUMANTE* WHITE WINE PROSECCO. WHEN SITTING IN A VENETIAN *PIAZZA* WATCHING THE WORLD GO BY, THIS IS THE ONLY WINE TO DRINK.

RICE ARRIVED IN ITALY ABOUT A THOUSAND YEARS AGO — IT IS BELIEVED TO BE YET
ANOTHER ARAB INTRODUCTION — AND WAS CULTIVATED IN THE FLAT PLAINS OF THE
PO VALLEY. THE MOST INTERESTING RICE RECIPES COME FROM THE NORTH, BUT IT IS
ALSO NOW WIDELY USED IN THE SOUTH TOO.

MANY TYPES OF RISOTTO RICE ARE GROWN IN ITALY. THERE ARE FOUR FORMAL
GRADES, RANGING FROM SHORT-GRAIN TO LONG-GRAIN: *COMMUNE* (COMMON),
SEMIFINO (SEMI-FINE), *FINO* (FINE) AND *SUPERFINO* (SUPER-FINE). EACH OF THESE
BOASTS A NUMBER OF VARIANTS. MOST RISOTTO RICES ARE *SUPERFINO*, WITH LONG
GRAINS. ARBORIO AND CARNAROLI ARE *SUPERFINO*, WHILE VIALONE NANO, ALTHOUGH
POPULAR AND OFTEN RECOMMENDED FOR RISOTTO, IS A SHORTER-GRAINED *SEMIFINO*.

THE ESSENCE OF A RISOTTO RICE IS ITS ABILITY TO RELEASE ITS STARCH AND
ABSORB FLAVOURS WHILE REMAINING *AL DENTE* IN THE MIDDLE. I THINK VIALONE
NANO DOES THIS BEST; IF YOU HOLD A RAW GRAIN OF IT UP TO THE LIGHT YOU CAN
SEE THE PLUMPNESS OF THE STARCH AT THE SIDES AROUND THE CENTRAL KERNEL.
THIS MAKES FOR A BETTER *CREMA*, THE CREAMINESS WHICH DEFINES THE BEST RISOTTO.

riso

RICE

THIS SOUP COMES FROM THE HOME OF ITALIAN RICE, THE VALLEY OF THE PO IN THE
VENETO. IT IS HEART-WARMING AND SATISFYING, SOMETHING FOR A REALLY COLD
WINTER'S DAY. *MINESTRONE* MEANS A MIXTURE, OR HOTCHPOTCH, AND VIRTUALLY
ANYTHING CAN GO IN THIS SOUP. HERE THE RICE GIVES SUBSTANCE, THE POTATOES
THICKNESS, AND THE CELERY CRISPNESS.

minestra di riso e sedano

RICE AND CELERY SOUP

SERVES 4

450G (1LB) WHITE CELERY

125G (4½OZ) FLOURY POTATOES

2.2 LITRES (4 PINTS) VEGETABLE BROTH
   (SEE PAGE 188)

4 TBSP OLIVE OIL

25G (1OZ) UNSALTED BUTTER

1 SMALL ONION, PEELED AND FINELY CHOPPED

2 GARLIC CLOVES, PEELED AND FINELY CHOPPED

A HANDFUL OF FRESH FLAT-LEAF PARSLEY,
   CHOPPED

125G (4½OZ) ITALIAN RICE, PREFERABLY
   VIALONE NANO

TO SERVE

2 TBSP EXTRA VIRGIN OLIVE OIL

FRESHLY GRATED PARMESAN CHEESE

1   Remove the inside leaves from the celery. Wash, dry and chop
    and set aside for garnish. Wash the rest of the celery and cut
    half of it into 1cm (½in) pieces.

2   Peel the potatoes and cut into similar pieces. Put both
    chopped vegetables in a heavy pot with half the broth and half
    the olive oil. Bring to the boil and simmer gently until the
    vegetables are cooked.

3   Put the contents of the pan through a food mill or food
    processor. Wash the saucepan.

4   Put the remaining olive oil and the butter into the pan and
    sauté the onion for about 10 minutes. Cut the remaining
    celery into 2.5cm (1in) long pieces and add to the pan with
    the garlic and parsley. Add the potato and celery purée to the
    pot, mix well, then pour in the remaining broth gradually,
    mixing well. Bring to the boil. Now add the rice, give a good
    stir and let it cook until tender (about 15 minutes).

5   Ladle the soup into bowls, sprinkle with the celery leaves and
    the extra virgin olive oil, and serve with grated Parmesan.

THESE RICE BALLS ARE ORIGINALLY FROM SICILY, BUT ARE NOW SEEN IN SNACK
BARS ALL OVER ITALY. THE MOST FAMOUS ARE THE *SUPPLÍ DI TELEFONO*, WHICH
HAVE A PIECE OF MOZZARELLA AT THEIR HEART; THIS TURNS INTO LONG STRINGS
AFTER COOKING. *SUPPLÍ* CAN COME IN MANY GUISES: VERY SMALL AS CANAPÉS, OR
LARGE TO ECHO THE MOUNTAINS; AND THEY CAN ALSO CONTAIN MEAT.

supplí di riso

RICE BALLS

MAKES 8, TO SERVE 4

800ML (28FL OZ) VEGETABLE BROTH
   (SEE PAGE 188)

55G (2OZ) UNSALTED BUTTER

275G (9½OZ) RISOTTO RICE, SUCH AS
   VIALONE NANO, CARNAROLI OR ARBORIO

175G (6OZ) MOZZARELLA CHEESE, CUT INTO
   SMALL CUBES

6 SHALLOTS, PEELED AND FINELY CHOPPED

A HANDFUL OF MIXED FRESH HERBS, SUCH AS
   PARSLEY, BASIL AND OREGANO, CHOPPED

FINELY GRATED ZEST OF 1 LARGE UNWAXED
   ORANGE

6 TBSP FRESHLY GRATED PARMESAN CHEESE

SEA SALT AND FRESHLY GROUND BLACK PEPPER

1 LARGE EGG, LIGHTLY BEATEN

55G (2OZ) FRESH BREADCRUMBS

6 TBSP OLIVE OIL FOR FRYING

1 Put the broth in a saucepan and heat until almost boiling, then reduce the heat until barely simmering.

2 Melt the butter in a wide saucepan. Add the rice and stir, using a wooden spoon, until the grains are well coated and glistening (about 1 minute). Add a ladleful of hot broth and simmer, stirring until it has all been absorbed. Continue to add the broth at intervals and cook as before, until all the liquid has been absorbed and the rice is tender but still firm — *al dente* — about 18-20 minutes. Remove from the heat.

3 Add the mozzarella, shallots, mixed herbs, orange zest, Parmesan, and some salt and pepper to the rice. Mix well, and let it cool. The rice is easier to handle and shape when it's cold.

4 Using your hands, shape the flavoured rice into eight balls. Dip each one into the beaten egg and coat well, then roll them in the breadcrumbs, pressing crumbs on to any uncovered area.

5 Heat the oil in a frying pan, add the rice balls — in batches if necessary — and cook until they are golden on all sides (about 8 minutes).

6 Drain well on kitchen paper. Serve hot or cold.

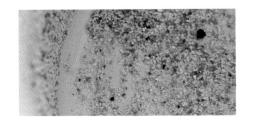

THIS CAKE IS FROM THE VENETO AND DISPLAYS MANY VENETIAN CULINARY CHARACTERISTICS – IN PARTICULAR THE USE OF RICE, DRIED FRUIT AND CANDIED PEEL. THIS IS BASICALLY A COLD RICE PUDDING THAT IS TRANSFORMED INTO A PUDDING-CAKE, AND IT IS DELICIOUS SERVED WITH A STRONG BLACK ESPRESSO – BUT YOU'LL ONLY NEED A TINY SLIVER OF THE CAKE. YOU COULD ADD SOME NUTS IF YOU PREFERRED.

torta campagnola

RICE CAKE

SERVES 10

150G (5½OZ) UNSALTED BUTTER

25G (1OZ) FINE BREADCRUMBS, TOASTED

115G (4OZ) RAISINS

2 TBSP MARSALA WINE

200ML (7FL OZ) MILK

200ML (7FL OZ) WATER

115G (4OZ) CASTER SUGAR

FINELY GRATED ZEST OF 2 UNWAXED LEMONS

½ TSP SALT

175G (6OZ) ARBORIO RICE

115G (4OZ) CANDIED PEEL, WHOLE IDEALLY

2 LARGE FREE-RANGE EGGS, SEPARATED

1 TBSP VANILLA EXTRACT

1 Grease a 1.1 litre (2 pint) ovenproof pudding basin with 15g (½oz) of the butter. Coat the basin with the breadcrumbs, shaking out the excess. Put in the fridge until ready to fill. (I have made this dish in a tin as well.)

2 In a small bowl, soak the raisins in the Marsala for at least 30 minutes.

3 In a large saucepan mix together the milk, water, sugar, lemon zest and salt. Bring the mixture to the boil, add the rice and simmer for 12-15 minutes. Turn into a bowl and leave to cool slightly. Preheat the oven to 180°C (350°F) gas mark 4.

4 Finely chop the candied peel and then melt the remaining butter. Add the peel to the rice with the egg yolks, vanilla extract, melted butter and the raisins and Marsala, and mix.

5 Whisk the egg whites until stiff, then fold into the rice mixture. Spread the rice evenly in the prepared basin. Bake for 40-50 minutes, until golden. Leave to cool. When cold, invert the cake on to a serving plate, cut into slim wedges and serve.

HERBS ARE A CORNERSTONE OF ITALIAN COOKING. SOFT HERBS ARE SOFTER IN LEAF
AND STALK THAN HARDY HERBS, AND MORE VULNERABLE TO TEMPERATURE.

THERE ARE TWO MAJOR TYPES OF BASIL IN ITALY: *LATTUGA* (LETTUCE-LEAF),
WHICH HAS HUGE LEAVES; AND THE SMALL-LEAVED *GENOVESE*. THE FORMER IS USED
IN SALADS OR ADDED TO A SAUCE AT THE END OF COOKING (THE HUGE FLAVOUR
BECOMES FUGITIVE WHEN COOKED); THE LATTER IS MOST FAMOUSLY USED IN PESTO.

PARSLEY – FLAT-LEAF OR CONTINENTAL RATHER THAN CURLY – IS USED AS A
SEASONING IN ITALIAN COOKING IN THE WAY YOU MIGHT USE SALT. IT ADDS COLOUR,
TEXTURE AND FLAVOUR. THE SAME CAN BE SAID OF CHIVES, WHICH GIVE A SUBTLE
ONION FLAVOUR; I LIKE THEM IN RAVIOLI (SEE PAGE 154) AND ON TOMATO BRUSCHETTA.

OREGANO AND ITS MORE DOMESTICATED COUSIN MARJORAM CAN BE FOUND WILD
IN THE MEDITERRANEAN, AND THEIR MINTY FRESHNESS ADDS TANG TO MANY DISHES.
MINT IS USED IN MANY WAYS, WITH VEGETABLES (IT'S WONDERFUL WITH COURGETTES
AND POTATOES), WITH FISH, IN SAUCES AND, IN EXTRACTED FORM, IN CONFECTIONERY
AND DRINKS.

erbe tenere

SOFT HERBS

GNOCCHI, OR LITTLE DUMPLINGS, ARE INCREDIBLY VERSATILE, AND COME FROM THE
NORTH (PROBABLY AN AUSTRIAN INFLUENCE). THEY CAN BE MADE FROM A VARIETY
OF INGREDIENTS – FROM SEMOLINA, POTATO AND PUMPKIN – BUT THESE RICOTTA
ONES ARE PROBABLY THE LIGHTEST OF ALL. I SERVE THEM REGULARLY WHEN I'M
TEACHING IN ITALY, AND THEY ARE ALWAYS DEVOURED IN A FLASH!

gnocchi di ricotta al basilico

RICOTTA DUMPLINGS WITH FRESH BASIL

SERVES 6

400G (14OZ) RICOTTA CHEESE

3 LARGE EGGS

100G (3½OZ) PLAIN FLOUR, PLUS EXTRA
    FOR SPRINKLING

6 TBSP FRESHLY GRATED PARMESAN CHEESE

55G (2OZ) FRESH BREADCRUMBS

A PINCH OF FRESHLY GRATED NUTMEG

SEA SALT AND FRESHLY GROUND BLACK PEPPER

25G (1OZ) BUTTER

115G (4OZ) FRESH BASIL, TORN

55G (2OZ) PINE NUTS, TOASTED

1   Mash the ricotta with the eggs, flour, 4 tbsp of the Parmesan,
    the breadcrumbs, nutmeg and some salt and pepper, and mix
    well. Add more flour if necessary to form a thick dough.

2   Sprinkle the work surface with flour then, using your hands,
    shape the dough into balls about the size of a walnut and roll
    in the flour.

3   Fill a large pan with water, bring to the boil, and carefully
    drop in the dumplings. Keep the water barely simmering until
    they rise to the surface. Using a slotted spoon, carefully lift
    the dumplings out and place on a serving dish.

4   Melt the butter and pour over the dumplings. Sprinkle with
    the basil and pine nuts and the remaining Parmesan cheese.
    Serve hot.

ravioli di patate e erbe

HERBED POTATO RAVIOLI

SERVES 6

PASTA

150G (5½OZ) FINE SEMOLINA

150G (5½OZ) ITALIAN '00' PLAIN FLOUR

A PINCH OF SALT

1 DSP OLIVE OIL

3 LARGE EGGS

STUFFING

350G (12OZ) FLOURY POTATOES

4 TBSP OLIVE OIL

1 SMALL ONION, PEELED AND FINELY CHOPPED

SEA SALT AND FRESHLY GROUND BLACK PEPPER

1 LARGE EGG YOLK

1 TBSP EACH OF CHOPPED FRESH CHIVES AND
    TORN BASIL LEAVES

2 TBSP CHOPPED FRESH MARJORAM

1 TSP FRESHLY GRATED NUTMEG

3 TBSP FRESHLY GRATED PARMESAN CHEESE

TO SERVE

55G (2OZ) UNSALTED BUTTER

1 TSP GROUND CINNAMON

25G (1OZ) PARMESAN CHEESE SHAVINGS

1   First make the pasta. Combine the flours and salt on the work surface. Make a well in the centre and put in the oil and eggs. Using a fork, break the eggs in as if making scrambled eggs and, with the side of your hand, flick in the flour to form a paste. Add more flour if it is too sticky.

2   Knead the dough for a generous 10 minutes, until it is strong and feels like silk. Wrap it in clingfilm and put aside to rest for at least 20 minutes while you prepare the stuffing.

3   Boil the potatoes in their skins. When cooked, peel them and purée them through a food mill or potato ricer into a bowl.

4   Heat the olive oil in a frying pan and sauté the onion for a few minutes to soften. Add to the potato purée with some salt and pepper. Mix in the egg yolk, herbs, nutmeg and Parmesan. Mix well to combine.

5   Unwrap the dough and place on a floured work surface. Divide into two pieces, and roll out one of the pieces to an ideal thickness of about 2mm (⅟₁₆in). Work one sheet of dough at a time, keeping the rest covered to stop it drying out. Cut the rolled-out sheet into 8cm (3¼in) squares. Place a mound of stuffing the size of a walnut on one square and cover with another square. Seal the dough all around with dampened fingers. Place each raviolo on clean linen towels. Repeat with the second sheet of dough.

5   When all the ravioli are made, bring a large saucepan of water to the boil. Add salt, then gently slide in half the ravioli, and cook for 4 minutes. When the pasta bobs to the top of the pan, retrieve it with a slotted spoon and transfer it, well-drained, to a large heated shallow dish. Cook the second batch and keep warm.

6   Melt the butter and cook until it begins to brown. Pour over the ravioli and sprinkle the cinnamon on top. Arrange Parmesan shavings on top and serve at once.

THIS DELICIOUS RECIPE IS VERY CHARACTERISTIC OF THE SOUTH, WHERE
COURGETTES GROW PROLIFICALLY. THE BEST POTATOES TO USE ARE ELVIRA AND
SPUNTA. IN ITALY THEY COME TO THE MARKETS COVERED IN THE DARK, SOUTHERN
VOLCANIC SOIL, WHICH GIVES THEM A FANTASTICALLY EARTHY FLAVOUR. THE
FLESH IS BRIGHT YELLOW. ALL THE POTATOES SHOULD BE THE SAME SIZE.

bianchetti di zucchini e patate novelle con erbe

NEW POTATOES WITH COURGETTES AND HERBS

SERVES 6

500G (1LB 2OZ) NEW ITALIAN POTATOES, PEELED

300ML (10FL OZ) DOUBLE CREAM

250ML (8FL OZ) WATER

4 SHALLOTS, PEELED AND FINELY CHOPPED

SEA SALT AND FRESHLY GROUND BLACK PEPPER

250G (9OZ) COURGETTES, SLICED INTO ROUNDS

JUICE OF 1 LEMON

A HANDFUL EACH OF FRESH FLAT-LEAF PARSLEY
   AND MINT, ROUGHLY CHOPPED

1   In a large saucepan, combine the potatoes, cream, water, shallots and some salt, and bring to the boil over a medium-high heat. Cover and continue to cook for 10 minutes.

2   Add the courgettes to the potatoes and cook for another 10 minutes.

3   Add the lemon juice, some pepper and the herbs. The potatoes should be tender and creamy. Season again as required and serve.

THE PROSECCO GRAPE AND THE WINE MADE FROM IT IN CONEGLIANO ARE FAMOUSLY AND INDISSOLUBLY ASSOCIATED WITH VENICE. THIS IS THE DRINK TO ORDER WHEN YOU POP INTO A BAR OR CAFÉ, EXHAUSTED, AFTER AN AFTERNOON OF WALKING. PROSECCO IS LIGHT, FRUITY AND ALMOST BUTTERY. IT CAN BE STILL, BUT IS MORE COMMONLY *FRIZZANTE* OR *SPUMANTE*. THE WINE SHOULD BE DRUNK YOUNG, AND YOU SHOULD ALWAYS APPRECIATE IT *IN SITU*: IT DOES NOT TRAVEL WELL AND, OF COURSE, YOU CAN'T EXPORT THAT VENETIAN ATMOSPHERE! THE FAMOUS HARRY'S BAR PRODUCED THE FIRST PROSECCO COCKTAIL, THE BELLINI, A MELD OF PROSECCO AND FRESH PEACH JUICE (BUT DON'T ASK FOR IT OUT OF SEASON). NAMED AFTER THE 15TH-CENTURY VENETIAN PAINTER, IT HAS BEEN FOLLOWED BY OTHER PAINTERLY COCKTAILS: THE TIZIANO (RED GRAPE JUICE), CANALETTO (PEAR JUICE) AND BOTTICELLI (STRAWBERRY JUICE) – ALTHOUGH THE LATTER WAS ACTUALLY A FLORENTINE RATHER THAN VENETIAN PAINTER.

prosecco

VENETIAN COCKTAILS

EACH OF THE FOLLOWING COCKTAILS SERVES 4

BOTTICELLI

400ML (14FL OZ) STRAWBERRY PURÉE, MADE
   FROM 2 PUNNETS STRAWBERRIES
1 BOTTLE GOOD-QUALITY PROSECCO

BELLINI

8 RIPE PEACHES, PEELED, STONED AND
   LIQUIDISED
1 BOTTLE GOOD-QUALITY PROSECCO

TIZIANO

400ML (14FL OZ) GRAPE JUICE
1 BOTTLE GOOD-QUALITY PROSECCO

CANALETTO

8 JUICY WILLIAM PEARS, PEELED, CORED AND
   LIQUIDISED
1 BOTTLE GOOD-QUALITY PROSECCO

Spring **Botticelli**
Place the strawberry purée in a carafe. Slowly add the wine and stir to blend. Pour into well-chilled glasses and serve.

Summer **Bellini**
Place the peach purée in a carafe. Slowly add the wine and stir to blend. Pour into well-chilled glasses and serve.

Autumn **Tiziano**
Unsweetened grape juice is available at many farmers' markets and health-food stores. To make your own, pass approximately 500g (1lb 2oz) of sweet red grapes through a mouli, or liquidise. Place the grape juice in a carafe. Slowly add the wine and stir to blend. Pour into well-chilled glasses and serve.

Winter **Canaletto**
Place the pear purée in a carafe. Slowly add the wine and stir to blend. Pour into well-chilled glasses and serve.

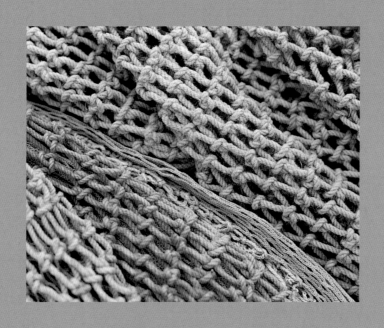

isole
islands

ITALY LIES ON THE CONJUNCTION OF TWO TECTONIC PLATES: THE AFRICAN AND THE EURASIAN. WHEN THE LAST MAJOR UPHEAVAL OCCURRED MILLIONS OF YEARS AGO, THE ALPS AND OTHER GREAT MOUNTAIN RANGES WERE FORMED AND THE CONTINENTS DRIFTED APART. THE VOLCANIC RIDGE THAT IS THE APENNINES FORMED THE MOUNTAINOUS BOOT SHAPE OF ITALY AND THE ISLANDS THAT SURROUND THE COUNTRY PRESUMABLY SPLIT FROM THE MAINLAND. PROBABLY BECAUSE OF THIS SHEARING AWAY, MOST OF ITALY'S ISLANDS CONSIST OF SIMILAR TERRAIN TO THE MAINLAND: PRIMARILY MOUNTAINS, AS WELL AS COASTS, FORESTS, WOODS AND SOME PLAINS. LAKES AND RIVERS ARE FEW, AND AS A RESULT MOST OF THE ISLANDS ARE DRY IN CLIMATE.

THE MAIN ITALIAN ISLANDS ARE, OF COURSE, SICILY AND SARDINIA. SICILY IS THE LARGEST ISLAND IN THE MEDITERRANEAN, CLOSELY FOLLOWED BY SARDINIA. BOTH ISLANDS LOOK LIKE A GIANT HAND HAS PLUCKED PIECES OF MOUNTAIN RANGE FROM THE SOUTHERN END OF THE ITALIAN BOOT AND SET THEM IN THE SEA SOME MILES AWAY. THE ROCK STRUCTURES, SOIL, VEGETATION AND COLOURS ARE REMINISCENT OF CALABRIA IN PARTICULAR, ALTHOUGH THE LIGHT IS CLEARER AND BRIGHTER, AS IS SO OFTEN THE CASE ON ISLANDS. THE CLIMATE IS DIFFERENT TOO, HOTTER AND DRIER THAN THE SOUTHERN PARTS OF MAINLAND ITALY.

THERE ARE A FEW ISLANDS TO THE WEST OF THE ITALIAN BOOT, NOTABLY ELBA, THE LARGEST ISLAND IN WHAT IS CALLED THE TUSCAN ARCHIPELAGO. NEAR TO THE FRENCH ISLAND OF CORSICA, WHERE EMPEROR NAPOLEON BONAPARTE WAS BORN, ELBA IS PRINCIPALLY FAMOUS AS THE PLACE OF HIS EXILE AFTER HIS ABDICATION. IT IS NOW A BEAUTIFUL TOURIST DESTINATION. FURTHER SOUTH ARE THE VOLCANIC ISCHIA, POPULAR BECAUSE OF ITS MILD CLIMATE AND MINERAL SPRINGS, AND CAPRI, NEAR THE BAY OF NAPLES. IT IS SAID THAT CAPRI HAS BEEN A HOLIDAY RESORT SINCE ROMAN TIMES, AND IT HAS WONDERFUL BEACHES, THE REMAINS OF THE EMPEROR TIBERIUS'S VILLAS AND *LA GROTTO AZZURA* (THE BLUE GROTTO), DISCOVERED AS

RECENTLY AS 1826. ACCESSIBLE ONLY FROM THE SEA, THE GROTTO IS MAGICAL, ACCLAIMED IN DOZENS OF POPULAR SONGS AND A MYRIAD POSTCARDS.

FURTHER SOUTH, OFF THE NORTH COAST OF SICILY, LIE THE LIPARI ISLANDS, ONCE KNOWN ROMANTICALLY AS THE AEOLIAN ISLANDS. THERE ARE SEVEN OF THESE, AMONG THEM LIPARI, STROMBOLI, VULCANO AND SALINA. ALL OF THEM ARE VOLCANIC, AND THE VOLCANOES ON STROMBOLI AND VULCANO ARE STILL ACTIVE. STROMBOLI'S CRATER CONTAINS MOLTEN LAVA, WHICH OCCASIONALLY SPILLS OVER INTO A MINOR FLOW, AND THE WHOLE AREA SMELLS OF THE SULPHUROUS COUGHS CONTINUALLY EMITTED FROM THE EARTH. SOUTH OF SICILY, AND ABOUT HALFWAY TO THE COAST OF TUNISIA, THE ISLAND OF PANTELLERIA (VOLCANIC ONCE AGAIN) SITS IN SOLITARY SPLENDOUR. FROM LIPARI AND PANTELLERIA COME SOME OF THE BEST CAPERS IN THE WORLD: FAT, JUICY AND AROMATIC FROM GROWING WILD IN THE HEAT OF THE SOUTHERN SUN.

THE COOKING OF THE ISLANDS, AS ELSEWHERE IN ITALY, HAS BEEN INFLUENCED BY INCOMING PEOPLES OVER THE CENTURIES, AMONG THEM THE GREEKS, PHOENICIANS, SARACENS OR ARABS, NORMANS (ORIGINALLY FROM SCANDINAVIA), FRENCH AND SPANISH. OFTEN THEY CAME FROM NEARER STILL, FROM ROME OR GENOA, BOTH THEN SEPARATE ACQUISITIVE CITY-STATES. THAT THE BASIS OF SARDINIAN AND SICILIAN COOKING IS VEGETABLES AND FISH IS DUE TO THE GREEKS, AND THE PASTA COMES FROM THE ITALIANS. THE ARABS INTRODUCED NEW FRUITS AND VEGETABLES, AMONG THEM AUBERGINES, SPINACH, APRICOTS, CITRUS, SUGAR AND ALMONDS, AND THEY TAUGHT THE ISLANDERS HOW TO PRESERVE AND DRY FRUIT. THE SARDINIAN *BURRIDA* OR FISH STEW IS CLOSELY RELATED TO THE GENOAN *BURIDDA* (AND INDEED TO THE PROVENÇAL *BOURRIDE*), AND A FAMOUS SARDINIAN FISH SOUP *CASSOLA* IS DERIVED FROM THE SPANISH. WITH SO MANY CULINARY THREADS, THE FOOD ON THE ITALIAN ISLANDS IS INTERESTING INDEED.

SARDINIA IS MAINLY MOUNTAINOUS, ALTHOUGH THERE IS A LARGE ALLUVIAL PLAIN IN
THE SOUTH-WEST, THE FERTILE CAMPIDANO, WHERE CEREALS, FRUITS, VINES AND
OLIVES ARE CULTIVATED. AFTER BEING SETTLED BY WAVES OF INVADERS, SARDINIA
WAS CEDED TO THE NORTHERN PIEDMONTESE KINGDOM OF SAVOY IN 1720. THERE ARE
TWO DISTINCT CUISINES ON THE ISLAND: THAT OF THE COASTS, WHICH IS WHERE THE
INCOMERS – OLD AND NEW – SETTLED; AND THAT OF THE INTERIOR, TO WHICH THE
NATIVE SARDINIANS RETREATED. THE COOKING OF THE COASTS REFLECTS MANY
INFLUENCES, AND SPECIALITIES INCLUDE TUNA (A MAJOR INDUSTRY), LOBSTER AND
BUTTARIGA OR BOTTARGA (DRIED GREY MULLET OR TUNA ROE). AWAY FROM THE
COAST, MYRTLE (USED IN LIQUEURS) IS A MAJOR FLAVOURING. CHEESE IS MADE IN
THE MOUNTAINS, PARTICULARLY THE FAMOUS PECORINO SARDO AND RICOTTA CHEESES.
THE SARDINIANS ALSO EAT A LOT OF FETA, A GREEK INFLUENCE PRESUMABLY.

PARSLEY IS THOUGHT TO BE ORIGINALLY NATIVE TO SARDINIA, SAFFRON IS WIDELY
GROWN, AND HUGE SALT LAGOONS NEAR CALIGARI PROVIDE SEA SALT FOR THE REST
OF ITALY.

sardegna

SARDINIA

WILD MYRTLES COVER SARDINIA, AND EVERY HOUSEHOLD THERE WILL HAVE ITS OWN SPECIAL BLEND FOR A LIQUEUR SUCH AS THIS. IN ITALY WE BELIEVE THAT LIQUEURS ARE GOOD FOR THE DIGESTION, AND WE MAKE THOUSANDS OF THEM FROM WALNUTS, HAZELNUTS, FRUITS AND LEMONS. MANY OF THESE LIQUEURS ARE NOW PRODUCED COMMERCIALLY. IF YOU CAN'T GET WILD MYRTLES, A SIMILAR AND EQUALLY DELICIOUS LIQUEUR CAN BE MADE IN THE SAME WAY FROM BLACKCURRANTS.

licore di mirtilli

MYRTLE LIQUEUR

MAKES ABOUT 4 LITRES (7 PINTS)

600G (1LB 5OZ) RIPE MYRTLE BERRIES

1 LITRE (1¾ PINTS) VODKA

500G (1LB 2OZ) CASTER SUGAR, OR

   600G (1LB 5OZ) HONEY

2 LITRES (3½ PINTS) WATER

1 Clean the berries. Place them in a container of dark glass with the alcohol and leave them to infuse for about 15 days.

2 When the time is up, strain and filter, pressing down on the berries to release the rich flavour. Discard the berries.

3 To make the syrup, dissolve the sugar or honey in 2 litres (3½ pints) of water in a pan over a gentle heat (about 10 minutes). Stir gently until the sugar has dissolved completely. Leave to cool.

4 Add the cold sugar syrup to the berry-infused alcohol and pour the liqueur into dark glass bottles.

5 Consume after 10 days.

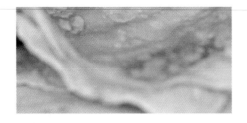

THIS IS NOW FAMILIAR TO US ALL AS A SPECIAL SARDINIAN BREAD. IT IS KNOWN AS *CARTA DI MUSICA* BECAUSE IT SHOULD BE THIN ENOUGH FOR YOU TO READ MUSIC THROUGH. BASICALLY, IT IS A FOOD FOR THE SHEPHERDS: THEY MIGHT SOFTEN IT IN EWES' MILK; CRUMBLE IT UP AND DRIZZLE WITH HONEY FOR BREAKFAST; OR SOFTEN IT IN WATER AND FILL IT WITH VEGETABLES BEFORE BAKING IT OVER THE FIRE AS A PANCAKE FOR LUNCH.

carasau

MUSIC SHEET BREAD

SERVES 8

10G (¼OZ) FRESH YEAST

1 DSP COARSE SALT

1KG (2¼LB) DURUM WHEAT FLOUR

1   Dissolve the yeast and the salt separately in 2 tbsp lukewarm water each. Heat 300ml (10fl oz) water to body temperature. Put the flour on the work surface and make a well in the middle. Add the yeast to the well with the salt water and the water. Knead to obtain a soft damp, smooth dough.

3   Shape eight balls of about 8cm (3¼ in) in diameter, cover, and leave to rise for about 4 hours in a dry place. Preheat the oven to 200°C (400°F) gas mark 6.

4   Roll out the individual pieces of dough, keeping them constantly floured so they do not stick, to obtain circles of about 2-3mm (¾-1in) thickness and 40cm (16in) in diameter. Cook the sheets of dough, one on top of the other – all eight at the same time – in the preheated oven and separate them only when they begin to swell.

5   At this point the bread is called *lentie* (*lentie* means soft, and at this stage the bread can be used as a pancake). To make *carasau* bread, replace the sheets separately in the oven until they are dry and crunchy (about 5 minutes).

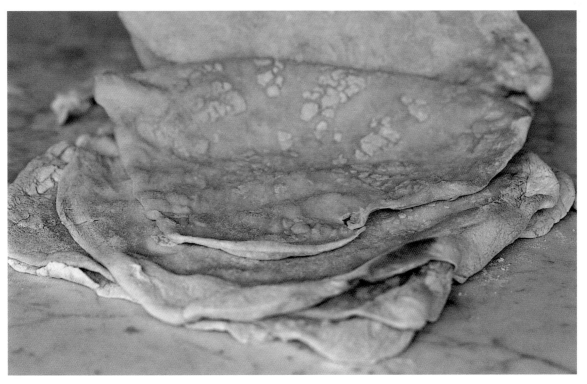

SARDINIA IS PREDOMINANTLY SHEPHERDING COUNTRY. IN ITS HIGH BLEAK
MOUNTAINS MANY LOCAL PRODUCTS ARE USED IN COOKING, PARTICULARLY WILD
GREENS AND HERBS. THIS SOUP IS TRADITIONALLY MADE WITH THE SMALL WILD
FENNEL THAT GROWS IN ABUNDANCE EVERYWHERE, BUT CULTIVATED FENNEL CAN
BE USED AS A SUBSTITUTE.

minestra con finocchi

FENNEL SOUP

SERVES 6

4 LARGE FENNEL BULBS

1 TBSP OLIVE OIL

1.5 LITRES (2¾ PINTS) VEGETABLE BROTH
  (SEE PAGE 188)

SEA SALT AND FRESHLY GROUND BLACK PEPPER

A HANDFUL OF FRESH FLAT-LEAF PARSLEY,
  CHOPPED

1 Clean the fennel bulbs and discard the stalks and tough outer
   layers. Slice the bulbs thinly, then chop finely.

2 Place the fennel in a saucepan with the olive oil and cook over
   a low heat for 10 minutes. Pour in the broth, season with salt
   and pepper and bring to a simmer.

3 Simmer for 30 minutes, then pour the soup into a tureen.
   Sprinkle with parsley and serve.

IN SARDINIAN COOKING, MUCH USE IS MADE OF PULSES, AS THEY ARE SEEN AS A PROTEIN AND ENERGY FOOD. PULSES ARE OFTEN FLAVOURED WITH SAFFRON, WHICH GIVES THEM A CHEERFUL COLOUR, A WONDERFUL DEPTH OF FLAVOUR AND A WARMTH. SAFFRON IS PRODUCED BY DRYING THE STAMEN OF A CERTAIN TYPE OF CROCUS – THERE ARE ONLY THREE IN EACH FLOWER, AND THEY ARE HAND-PICKED, SO ONE CAN UNDERSTAND WHY THE SPICE IS SO EXPENSIVE!

ceci allo zafferano

CHICKPEAS WITH SAFFRON

SERVES 6

500G (1LB 2OZ) DRIED CHICKPEAS

3 TBSP OLIVE OIL

1 ONION, PEELED AND CHOPPED

6 RIPE TOMATOES, SKINNED AND CHOPPED

A PINCH OF DRIED CHILLI (*PEPERONCINO*),
    CRUMBLED

SEA SALT AND FRESHLY GROUND BLACK PEPPER

6 SAFFRON STRANDS

1   Soak the chickpeas in cold water, covered, for 12 hours.

2   Drain the chickpeas and place in a saucepan. Add plenty of water and bring to a boil. Boil vigorously for 10 minutes, skim the top, then turn the heat down as low as possible and cook for 30 minutes, until tender. Drain.

3   Heat the olive oil in a pan over a medium heat. Add the onion and cook until translucent. Add the chickpeas, then the tomatoes and chilli. Season with salt and pepper and simmer for 20 minutes.

4   Dissolve the saffron in a little water and add to the pan. Mix well. Transfer to a bowl and serve.

BOTTARGA, WHICH LOOKS LIKE A GREY-BROWN HARD SALAMI, IS ACTUALLY GREY
MULLET ROE PRESERVED IN SALT. YOU CAN GET TUNA BOTTARGA AS WELL AND,
ALTHOUGH I LIKE THEM BOTH, THE MULLET VERSION IS THOUGHT TO BE THE BEST.
IT CAN BE USED IN FINE SLICES OR GRATED TO ADD INTEREST TO SIMPLE PASTA
AND RICE DISHES. THE FLAVOUR IS VERY UNUSUAL, FISHY AND INTENSE.

spaghetti con bottarga

SPAGHETTI WITH BOTTARGA

SERVES 4

350G (12OZ) SPAGHETTI

SEA SALT AND FRESHLY GROUND BLACK PEPPER

3 DSP SARDINIAN OLIVE OIL

12 VERY THIN SLICES BOTTARGA

JUICE OF ½ LEMON

1 GARLIC CLOVE, PEELED AND FINELY CRUSHED

A HANDFUL OF FRESH FLAT-LEAF PARSLEY,
   ROUGHLY CHOPPED

1   Cook the spaghetti in plenty of boiling salted water.

2   In the meantime, heat a little olive oil in a small saucepan
    and add the bottarga. Add some of the cooking water from
    the pasta pot. As soon as the bottarga has dissolved, add the
    lemon juice.

3   Strain the pasta and mix with the bottarga sauce. Dust with
    pepper, garlic and parsley, and serve immediately.

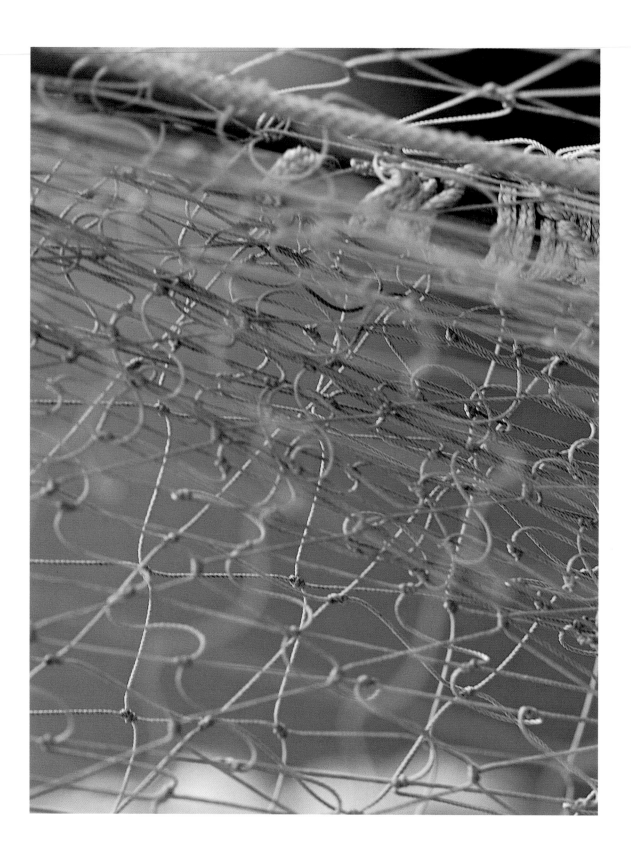

SEA URCHINS ARE LOOKED UPON AS TRUE FRUITS OF THE SEA, AND A REAL TREAT
IN SARDINIA. I REMEMBER THEM BEING SERVED IN HUGE PILES IN THE CENTRE OF
THE TABLE, THE BLACK SPIKY ORBS CUT IN HALF TO REVEAL THE VIOLENT ORANGE
OF THE INSIDES. THEY WERE EATEN FROM THE SHELL WITH A LITTLE OIL AND SALT
ON THEM. SAFFRON IS CHARACTERISTIC OF SARDINIAN COOKING, AND IT IS OFTEN
USED IN CONJUNCTION WITH FISH, AS HERE. SERVE THIS WONDERFUL SAUCE WITH
PASTA OR RICE.

salsa di ricci

SEA URCHIN SAUCE

SERVES 4

30 SEA URCHINS

400G (14OZ) RIPE TOMATOES

500ML (18FL OZ) VEGETABLE BROTH
   (SEE PAGE 188)

1 ONION, PEELED AND CHOPPED

2 TBSP OLIVE OIL

4 SAFFRON STRANDS, DISSOLVED IN A
   LITTLE WATER

2 GARLIC CLOVES, PEELED AND CHOPPED

A HANDFUL OF FRESH FLAT-LEAF PARSLEY,
   CHOPPED

SEA SALT AND FRESHLY GROUND BLACK PEPPER

1 Clean the sea urchins by extracting the inner part with a
   teaspoon. Skin the tomatoes, remove the seeds and chop the
   flesh into large pieces. Heat the broth.

2 Cook the chopped onion in the olive oil to soften a little, then
   add the tomatoes and cook lightly for 5 minutes. Add to the
   broth with the saffron. Add the urchin pulp, the garlic and
   parsley to form a sauce. Check the seasoning, heat through,
   and serve with bread.

THIS IS A TYPICAL SARDINIAN DISH, USING THE LOCAL PECORINO, WHICH IS MORE INTENSE IN FLAVOUR THAN ROMANO. IT OFTEN HAS WHOLE PEPPERCORNS IN IT, WHICH IS WONDERFUL. THE COMBINATION OF THE FAIRLY BLAND POTATO AND THE STRONG CHEESE IS A GOOD ONE. TO CREATE A VERY DIFFERENT TEXTURE, YOU COULD BOIL THESE AS YOU WOULD RAVIOLI INSTEAD OF BAKING THEM.

culingiones di patate

POTATO TARTS

SERVES 6 AS AN ANTIPASTO

PASTRY

500G (1LB 2OZ) ITALIAN '00' PLAIN FLOUR

250G (9OZ) UNSALTED BUTTER

1 TSP SEA SALT

FILLING

600G (1LB 5OZ) POTATOES

300G (10½OZ) PECORINO SARDO CHEESE,
    FRESHLY GRATED

2 GARLIC CLOVES, PEELED AND CRUSHED

A HANDFUL OF FRESH MINT, CHOPPED

SEA SALT AND FRESHLY GROUND BLACK PEPPER

TO SERVE

300G (10½OZ) TOMATO SAUCE (SEE PAGE 188)

100G (3½OZ) PECORINO SARDO CHEESE,
    FRESHLY GRATED

1 Make a well with the flour on a work surface, then add the butter and salt and work together with your fingers until the texture is like breadcrumbs. Add enough water to form a soft dough. Cover with a damp cloth and leave to rest for about 20 minutes.

2 Meanwhile boil the potatoes until tender, then peel and mash them. Add the cheese, garlic and mint and some salt and pepper to taste.

3 Preheat the oven to 200°C (400°F) gas mark 6.

4 Roll out the dough to obtain a thin sheet of pastry, and cut out 12 circles of about 7cm (2¾ in) in diameter. Drop a small quantity of potato mixture in the centre of the circles, fold them over and close them, pinching the edges.

5 Cook the *culingiones* in the preheated oven for about 20 minutes. Heat the tomato sauce, and drizzle over the pastries. Sprinkle with the grated cheese and serve.

THE PIZZA WAS BORN IN NAPLES, BUT IT HAS TRAVELLED ALL OVER MAINLAND ITALY AND THE ISLANDS. THIS ONE IS POPULAR IN SARDINIA AND ALONG THE RIVIERA. THE SALTINESS OF THE ANCHOVIES GOES WONDERFULLY WITH THE NEW SEASON'S TOMATOES – BUT DON'T USE ANY CHEESE; YOU DON'T NEED IT WITH FISH. THE PIZZA DOUGH IS SHORTER THAN OTHER DOUGHS.

pizza di sardegna

SARDINIAN PIZZA

SERVES 8

PIZZA DOUGH

15G (½OZ) FRESH YEAST

225G (8OZ) STRONG FLOUR, PLUS EXTRA
   FOR SPRINKLING

1 TSP SALT

65G (2¼OZ) BUTTER

1 LARGE EGG, BEATEN

OLIVE OIL

TOPPING

OLIVE OIL

750G (1LB 10OZ) ONIONS, PEELED AND FINELY
   SLICED

500G (1LB 2OZ) RIPE TOMATOES, SKINNED AND
   ROUGHLY CHOPPED

SEA SALT AND FRESHLY GROUND BLACK PEPPER

55G (2OZ) ANCHOVY FILLETS

A FEW BLACK OLIVES, HALVED AND STONED

A HANDFUL OF FRESH OREGANO

1   To make the dough, blend the yeast with 4 tbsp water at body temperature. Mix the flour and salt together in a large bowl, rub in the butter and make a well in the centre. Put in the egg and the yeast liquid and mix to a firm but pliable dough, adding more water if necessary. When the dough has come away cleanly from the sides of the bowl, turn out on to a floured surface and knead thoroughly for 10 minutes. Gather into a ball, place into a clean oiled bowl and cover and leave to rise until doubled in size (about 1½ hours).

2   When risen, turn the dough out on to a floured surface, divide into two and knead each piece lightly. Place in two well-oiled 20-23cm (8-9in) tins and press out with floured knuckles. Cover the tins and preheat the oven to 200°C (400°F) gas mark 6 while you prepare the toppings.

3   To make the topping, heat 5 tbsp of olive oil in a heavy pan and fry the onion gently, covered, stirring now and then, until soft (about 20 minutes). Add the tomatoes and seasoning and cook, uncovered, until the sauce is thick. Leave to become cold.

4   When cold, divide the topping between the pizzas, spreading it evenly. Criss-cross the surface with strips of anchovy and put halves of stoned olives in the spaces. Sprinkle with oregano and bake in the preheated oven for 25 minutes, until golden brown and bubbling.

SICILY CONSISTS PRINCIPALLY OF MOUNTAINS, AND MOUNT ETNA IS STILL ACTIVE. THE ARABS COLONISED THE ISLAND FOR TWO CENTURIES, AND THEIR INFLUENCE IS STILL APPARENT IN INGREDIENTS, AGRICULTURE, CULINARY TECHNIQUES AND DISHES.

PASTA IS THE BASIS OF SICILIAN COOKING, AND FISH DOMINATES. TUNA, SWORDFISH AND SARDINES ARE THE PRINCIPAL VARIETIES. A TYPICAL RECIPE IS *PASTA CON LE SARDE* (PASTA WITH SARDINES), WHICH ALSO CONTAINS FENNEL AND THE ARAB INGREDIENTS, RAISINS AND PINE NUTS. MANY SAVOURY DISHES ARE SWEETENED IN THIS WAY. CAPERS FEATURE TOO, AS THEY FLOURISH IN SICILY (AS IN NEARBY LIPARI AND PANTELLERIA). A TYPICAL SICILIAN VEGETABLE RECIPE WITH ARABIC OVERTONES (CAPERS, PINE NUTS ETC) IS *CAPONATA*, BASED ON AUBERGINES.

THE ARABS ALSO INTRODUCED MANY FRUIT AND NUT TREES, AND THE ISLAND IS FAMOUS FOR ITS CITRUS, FIGS, PINE NUTS AND ALMONDS. SORBETS AND ICE-CREAMS ARE FOREVER ASSOCIATED WITH SICILY, ANOTHER ARABIC IDEA, PARTLY BECAUSE THE ISLAND IS SO RICH IN THE BASIC INGREDIENTS. IN FACT, SWEET THINGS ARE A MAJOR FEATURE OF SICILIAN COOKING.

sicilia

SICILY

PANTELLERIA IS A SMALL ISLAND SOUTH-WEST OF SICILY, FAMOUS FOR ITS CAPERS, BOTH WILD AND CULTIVATED. THEY GROW PROLIFICALLY IN THE HOT, DRY CLIMATE, CREEPING AND CLIMBING OVER AND BETWEEN THE ROCKS. THEY HAVE A WONDERFUL MEDITERRANEAN AROMA AND FLAVOUR, WHICH IS BEST PRESERVED WHEN THEY ARE CURED IN SALT. THIS IS ITALY'S NIÇOISE SALAD, WITH ALL THE SAME WONDERFUL FLAVOURS.

insalata pantesca

CAPER SALAD

SERVES 6

55G (2OZ) PANTELLERIA CAPERS,
   OR JUST GOOD SALTED CAPERS

3 ITALIAN SPUNTA POTATOES, PEELED AND
   CUT INTO 2CM (¾IN) CUBES

SEA SALT AND FRESHLY GROUND BLACK PEPPER

2 FRESH SAGE LEAVES

4 PLUM TOMATOES, QUARTERED

1 RED ONION, PEELED AND SLICED INTO RINGS

1 X 400G TIN FINE TUNA IN OLIVE OIL

32 BLACK OLIVES, STONED

2 BUNCHES ROCKET

A HANDFUL OF FRESH BASIL LEAVES, TORN

DRESSING

5 TBSP SICILIAN EXTRA VIRGIN OLIVE OIL

1 TBSP RED WINE VINEGAR

1 Soak the capers in water for 20 minutes, changing the water two to three times, then drain.

2 Cover the potatoes, in a saucepan, with salted water and add the sage leaves. Bring to the boil, reduce the heat and simmer for about 5 minutes, until tender. Drain and set aside.

3 To make the dressing, in a small bowl whisk the extra virgin olive oil and vinegar together with some salt and pepper.

4 In a salad bowl, combine the capers, tomatoes, onion, tuna, olives, rocket and potatoes. Add the basil, drizzle with the dressing and serve.

THE BEST LOBSTERS ARE TINY AND SWEET AND ARE FOUND IN SICILY ON THE SOUTH-WEST COAST. THE RICHNESS OF THEIR FLAVOUR CONTRASTS WONDERFULLY WITH THE SIMPLICITY OF THE SPAGHETTI. TWIRL THE PASTA IN THE USUAL WAY, BUT DIVE IN WITH YOUR HANDS AS WELL – SOMETHING THE ITALIANS LOVE TO DO.

spaghetti con salsa di aragostine

SPAGHETTI WITH LOBSTER SAUCE

SERVES 4

3 SMALL LIVE LOBSTERS OR LOBSTER TAILS,
    WEIGHING ABOUT 400G (14OZ) EACH

3 TBSP OLIVE OIL

2 GARLIC CLOVES, PEELED AND CHOPPED

A GENEROUS PINCH OF DRIED CHILLI
    (*PEPERONCINO*), CRUMBLED

125ML (4FL OZ) DRY WHITE WINE

A HANDFUL OF FRESH FLAT-LEAF PARSLEY,
    ROUGHLY CHOPPED

SEA SALT AND FRESHLY GROUND BLACK PEPPER

350G (12OZ) SPAGHETTI

2 TBSP FINE SICILIAN EXTRA VIRGIN OLIVE OIL
    FOR DRIZZLING

1 Bring a pan of salted water to the boil and drop in the lobsters. Simmer for 12 minutes and leave to cool. Halve the lobsters and remove the flesh from the bodies, discarding the stomach sacs. Crack the pincers and remove the meat. Keep to one side.

2 Heat the olive oil in a sauté pan, then add the garlic and chilli. Sauté for a couple of minutes, then add the wine. Bring to the boil, add the cooked lobster meat and the parsley, and simmer for 4 more minutes. Season with salt and pepper.

3 Cook the spaghetti in plenty of boiling salted water until *al dente*, then drain. Toss with the lobster sauce, drizzle with good olive oil and serve at once.

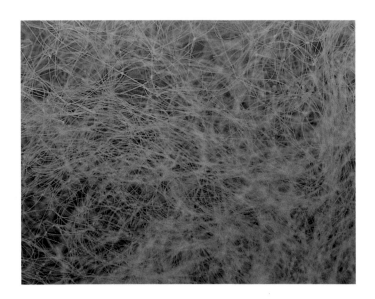

THE BEST SEA BASS COME FROM SICILY, THEY SAY, WHICH IS PROBABLY TRUE AS THERE THE SICILIANS EAT AND SLEEP FISH. I REMEMBER GOING TO A BUSINESS MEETING WITH MY FATHER ONCE, LURED BY THE PROMISE OF A WONDERFUL LUNCH. I WAS VERY YOUNG AND VERY SLEEPY, AND EVERY TIME I WOKE UP THEY WERE STILL TALKING ABOUT FOOD, FISH IN PARTICULAR! ONCE EATEN, THIS SIMPLE RECIPE IS NEVER FORGOTTEN, AND IT HAS BECOME A STAPLE PART OF THE REPERTOIRE OF MANY OF MY STUDENTS IN ITALY. JOHN DORY COULD BE PREPARED IN THE SAME WAY.

spigola 'al sale'

SEA BASS WITH SALT

SERVES 4-6

1 X 1KG (2¼LB) SEA BASS, SCALED AND GUTTED

1KG (2¼LB) LARGE-GRAIN SALT

TO SERVE

EXTRA VIRGIN OLIVE OIL FOR DRIZZLING
    (OPTIONAL)

1 LEMON FOR SQUEEZING (OPTIONAL)

1   Preheat the oven to 200°C (400°F) gas mark 6.

2   Wash and clean the fish thoroughly without removing the scales. Distribute a 1cm (½in) thick layer of salt in a baking tray. Place the fish on the salt and cover completely with the remaining salt. The fish should be completely hidden by the salt. Put the fish in the oven for 25 minutes.

3   Before serving, remove the salt carefully, extracting the fish, which should be served as it is with no seasoning. However, if desired, a thin drizzle of extra virgin olive oil can be served with the fish, as can lemon juice.

This is probably the most 'chefy' recipe in the whole book, but it's certainly worth making – especially for a dinner party. Swordfish are found in abundance in the waters around Sicily, and they are served in a variety of ways. Here the influence is definitely Arabic, with the capers, spices, dried fruit, pine nuts and olives.

pesce spada ripieno alla siciliana

SICILIAN STUFFED SWORDFISH WITH CHERRY TOMATO SAUCE

SERVES 4

2 SWORDFISH STEAKS, ABOUT 5CM (2IN) THICK

3 TBSP RAISINS

3 TBSP PINE NUTS

250G (9OZ) COARSE ITALIAN BREAD, CRUSTS
    REMOVED, CUT INTO 2.5CM (1IN) DICE

4 TBSP EACH OF DRY WHITE WINE AND FISH
    BROTH (SEE PAGE 189)

4 TBSP COARSELY CHOPPED FENNEL FRONDS

3 ANCHOVY FILLETS, MASHED

1 TBSP PLUS 1 TSP SALTED CAPERS, DRAINED
    AND RINSED

A PINCH EACH OF GROUND CINNAMON AND
    FRESHLY GRATED NUTMEG

SEA SALT AND FRESHLY GROUND BLACK PEPPER

OLIVE OIL

ITALIAN '00' PLAIN FLOUR FOR DREDGING

A PINCH OF CRUSHED DRIED CHILLI
    (*PEPERONCINO*)

400G (14OZ) CHERRY TOMATOES, QUARTERED

200G (7OZ) CANNED CHOPPED TOMATOES

100G (3½OZ) GAETA OLIVES, STONED AND
    COARSELY CHOPPED

1 On a work surface, cut the swordfish steaks in half crosswise, then cut each half horizontally into four slices of 13 x 7.5cm (5 x 3in). Cover each slice with clingfilm and gently pound the slices until they are 3mm (⅛in) thick. Cover and refrigerate.

2 In a heatproof bowl, soak the raisins in hot water until softened (about 10 minutes), then drain. In a small pan toast the pine nuts, shaking the pan until lightly browned (about 2 minutes).

3 In a shallow dish, soak the bread in the wine and fish stock for 10 minutes. Gently squeeze the bread almost dry. Finely chop the bread and transfer to a bowl. Gently stir in 2 tbsp each of the raisins and pine nuts, 2 tbsp of the fennel fronds, two-thirds of the anchovy fillets, the 1 tbsp capers, the cinnamon, nutmeg, and some salt and pepper.

4 Lay the swordfish slices out on the work surface and season with salt and pepper. Spoon about 1 dsp of the filling into the centre of each slice and roll up like a cigar, folding in the sides as you go. Secure each roll with a wooden toothpick.

5 In a frying pan, heat 1cm (½in) of olive oil. Lightly dredge the swordfish rolls with flour. Fry four of the rolls at a time over a moderately high heat until golden brown (about 2 minutes each side), then transfer to a plate. Repeat with the remaining rolls. Wipe out the pan.

6   In the same pan heat 2 tbsp of olive oil, add the chilli, the
    remaining anchovy fillet and remaining capers, and cook for
    30 seconds. Add the cherry tomatoes and canned tomatoes and
    cook over a low heat until thickened (about 15 minutes). Stir in
    the olives, 1 tbsp of the fennel fronds and the remaining pine
    nuts and raisins. Season with salt and pepper.

7   Add the swordfish rolls to the sauce. Cover and simmer over a
    low heat, turning the rolls a few times until heated through
    (about 3 minutes). Set the rolls on each plate, remove the
    toothpicks and spoon some sauce on top.

8   Garnish with the remaining fennel fronds. Serve immediately.

SICILY IS FAMOUS FOR ITS SORBETS, AND INDEED FOR ITS CLEMENTINES. THE FLAVOUR OF THE FRUIT IS SO MUCH STRONGER AND NICER THAN THAT OF THE SATSUMAS YOU GET FROM SPAIN. IF YOU CAN'T GET HOLD OF CLEMENTINES OR THEIR JUICE, USE BLOOD ORANGE JUICE INSTEAD (BLOOD ORANGES ALSO COME FROM SICILY). THE VIN SANTO HERE ACTUALLY COMES FROM TUSCANY, BUT IT IS NOW FOUND ALL OVER THE COUNTRY.

sorbetti di clementina

CLEMENTINE SORBET

SERVES 8

500ML (18FL OZ) CLEMENTINE JUICE

FINELY GRATED ZEST OF 3 CLEMENTINES,
    PREFERABLY ORGANIC AND UNWAXED

1 TBSP VIN SANTO

2 TBSP LEMON JUICE

SYRUP

240G (8½OZ) CASTER SUGAR

1   Mix together the clementine juice, zest, vin santo, 300ml (10fl oz) of water and lemon juice and chill.

2   Make the syrup by bringing 350ml (12fl oz) of water and the sugar to the boil. Quickly lower the heat to a simmer, and simmer for 5 minutes to melt the sugar. Remove from the heat and allow to cool before chilling well.

3   Mix the cold syrup with the cold juices and process in an ice-cream machine or place in a freezer compartment for 3 hours. Fork over and re-freeze for an hour.

appendix

MAKES ABOUT 1 LITRE (1¾ PINTS)

40G (1½OZ) UNSALTED BUTTER

1 TBSP OLIVE OIL

1 LARGE ONION, PEELED AND COARSELY
   CHOPPED

4 LEEKS, COARSELY CHOPPED

2 CARROTS, COARSELY CHOPPED

2 CELERY STALKS, COARSELY CHOPPED

2 HERB FENNEL STALKS, COARSELY CHOPPED

3 GARLIC CLOVES, PEELED AND CRUSHED

A HANDFUL OF FRESH FLAT-LEAF PARSLEY,
   CHOPPED

4 FRESH BAY LEAVES

2 SPRIGS FRESH THYME

MAKES 300ML (10FL OZ)

720G (1LB 10OZ) FRESH RIPE TOMATOES,
   OR 600G (1LB 5OZ) CANNED ITALIAN PLUM
   TOMATOES

1½ TBSP OLIVE OIL

1 ONION, PEELED AND FINELY CHOPPED

2 GARLIC CLOVES, PEELED AND CRUSHED

200ML (7FL OZ) VEGETABLE BROTH
   (SEE PAGE 188) OR WATER

1 TBSP TOMATO PURÉE

A PINCH OF CASTER SUGAR

SEA SALT AND FRESHLY GROUND BLACK PEPPER

1½ TBSP DRY WHITE WINE

Brodo di verdura *Vegetable broth*

This is the broth to use for soups, risotto and sauces. It is
subtly and deliciously flavoured.

1 Melt the butter and olive oil in a large, heavy-based saucepan.
   Add the onion, and fry for 2 minutes, then add all the
   remaining ingredients. Cook, stirring constantly, until
   softened but not browned.

2 Add 3 litres (5½ pints) of water and bring to the boil.
   Reduce the heat, cover, and simmer for about 1½ hours.
   Allow to cool.

3 Return the pan to the heat and simmer for 15 minutes. Strain
   the broth and return to the cleaned pan, discarding the solids.
   Boil rapidly until reduced by half, then use as needed or let
   cool and keep in the fridge for up to three days or freeze.

Salsa di tomate *Tomato sauce*

There are a number of tomato sauces throughout the book,
but this is the classic one, great to make when you have a glut
of tomatoes. Keep it in the freezer ready for use.

1 If using fresh tomatoes, blanch them to loosen the skins, then
   remove the skins and seeds and chop the flesh coarsely. Drain
   the canned tomatoes and chop coarsely.

2 Heat the olive oil in a heavy-based saucepan and sauté the
   onion gently for 5 minutes, until softened.

3 Add the tomatoes and garlic, cover and cook over a gentle
   heat for 10 minutes, stirring occasionally.

4 Add the broth or water, tomato purée, sugar and other
   seasonings. Half cover the pan and simmer for 20 minutes,
   stirring occasionally.

5 Sieve the tomato mixture into a clean pan, bring to the boil
   and add the wine, then use as required, or freeze.

MAKES ABOUT 450ML (15FL OZ)

25G (1OZ) UNSALTED BUTTER

55G (2OZ) ONIONS, PEELED AND CHOPPED

675G-900G (1½-2LB) WHITE FISH BONES,
    CLEANED

2 SPRIGS FRESH THYME

2 BAY LEAVES

1 CELERY STALK, CHOPPED

A HANDFUL OF FRESH FLAT-LEAF PARSLEY,
    LEAVES AND STALKS

1 TSP WHITE PEPPERCORNS

Brodo di pesce *Fish broth*

The Italians never allow anything to go to waste, particularly bones. Allied with other flavourings such as onion and herbs, the fish bones create a broth that is vital for soups, fish casseroles, fish risottos and sauces (never use oily fish bones for broth).

1 Melt the butter in a large saucepan, add the onions, and let them sweat for 5 minutes.

2 Add the fish bones and thyme, bay leaves, celery, parsley and peppercorns. Cook for 5 minutes, stirring constantly.

3 Add 1 litre (1¾ pints) water, bring to the boil, then reduce to a simmer for 20 minutes, uncovered.

4 Strain the stock through a conical sieve, cool and refrigerate (or freeze).

index